D0235783

RING WARS

300
200
150
100
50
0

RING WARS

A PICTORIAL HISTORY OF BOXING

HARRY MULLAN

First published in Great Britain in 1997 by
Parragon
Unit 13–17
Avonbridge Trading Estate
Atlantic Road
Avonmouth
Bristol BS11 9QD

Copyright © Parragon 1997

All rights reserved. No part of this publication may be reproduced, stored in a retrieval system or transmitted, in any form or by any means, electronic, mechanical, photocopying, recording or otherwise, without the prior permission of the copyright holder.

ISBN: 0-7525-2227-2

Conceived, designed and produced by Haldane Mason, London

Acknowledgements
Art Director: **Ron Samuels**
Editor: **Tessa Rose**
Picture Research: **Charles Dixon-Spain**

Colour reproduction by
Regent Publishing Services, Hong Kong

Printed in Italy

Page 1:
Roberto Duran, four-time world champion, loses on points to the Marvelous Marvin Hagler for the World Middleweight title.
Page 2:
Joe Frazier is given the evil eye by George Foreman before their 1973 bout in Jamaica.
Page 3:
Evander Holyfield climbs into the ring before his historic clash with 'Iron' Mike Tyson.

THE MEXICAN WARRIOR

JULIO CESAR CHAVEZ

HAND OF STONE

ROBERTO DURAN

BROWN BOMBER

JOE LOUIS

CONTENTS

PREFACE 6

THE POWER BROKERS 8
The Organizations 8

THE DEAL MAKERS 14
Rich Rose 14
Don King 14
Frank Warren 16
Bob Arum 17
Cedric Kushner 17
The Duva Family 17

MODERN GREATS 18
Alexis Arguello 20
Julio Cesar Chavez 22
Roberto Duran 24
Marvin Hagler 26
Thomas Hearns 28
Larry Holmes 30
Sugar Ray Leonard 32
Azumah Nelson 34
Eusebio Pedroza 36
Aaron Pryor 38

THE ENTERTAINERS 40
Riddick Bowe 42
Jorge Castro 42
Steve Collins 43
Oscar De La Hoya 43
Chris Eubank 44
Prince Naseem Hamed 44
Bernard Hopkins 45
Julian Jackson 45
Roy Jones 46
Lennox Lewis 46
Ricardo Lopez 47
Mike McCallum 47
Wayne McCullough 48
Terry Norris 48
Ike Quartey 49
Frankie Randall 49
Johnny Tapia 50
Felix Trinidad 50
Kosta Tszyu 51
Pernell Whitaker 51

THE LEGENDS 52
Muhammad Ali 54
Jack Dempsey 56
Joe Frazier 58
Jack Johnson 60
Sonny Liston 62
Joe Louis 64
Rocky Marciano 66
Mike Tyson 68

CLASSIC FIGHTS 70
Willie Pep vs Sandy Saddler 72
Carmen Basilio vs Sugar Ray Robinson 74
Joe Frazier vs Muhammad Ali 76
Muhammad Ali vs Joe Frazier 78
Roberto Duran vs Sugar Ray Leonard 80
Marvin Hagler vs Thomas Hearns 82
Barry McGuigan vs Eusebio Pedroza 84
Julio Cesar Chavez vs Meldrick Taylor 86
Nigel Benn vs Gerald McClellan 88
Evander Holyfield vs Mike Tyson 90

THE ARENAS 92

PICTURE CREDITS 96

PREFACE

More than 30 years ago , as a starry-eyed young boxing fan, I used to haunt the Fleet Street offices of *Boxing News* in my lunch-hour escape from a numbingly boring Civil Service job. I longed to be a boxing writer, but it seemed then a hopeless daydream. The late Tim Riley, editor at the time, was an easy-going and gentle man who tolerated my presence as I read through bound volumes of the magazine or chased obscure results for the boxers' career records which I endlessly compiled. The same could not be said of the proprietor, Vivian Brodsky, who found me there one lunchtime and ordered me to leave. 'Young man', he thundered, 'this is not a public reading room. Get out!' Brodsky would never know that the youngster he humilated that day would return in 1974 to join the staff and go on to become the second longest-serving editor in the paper's 88-year history. Sweet revenge.

I edited the paper for just over 19 years, from August 1977 until September 1996, and was lucky enough to see most of the great fights and outstanding performers of that colourful era. On the first of more than 40 American trips, I watched Muhammad Ali become champion for the third time in New Orleans in 1978, and I had a ring-apron position when Marvin Hagler and Thomas Hearns staged the greatest fight – and unquestionably the most exciting opening round – in boxing history. I can't claim to have known them all, as I tend to shun press lunches and the like, but I have met my share and it has always been a privilege.

Just as Nat Fleischer would always insist that the stars from the early years of his *Ring* magazine's life were better than any who came after them, so I refuse to believe that there have been, or will be, better or more consistently thrilling champions than Hagler, Ali, Duran, Leonard, Hearns, McGuigan, Nelson, Holmes, Tyson, Chavez or any of the other luminaries whose careers I have charted over the years.

Those years have been enormous fun, and it remains a source of joyous amazement to me that I am actually paid to sit at ringsides around the world. The novelty has never worn off: if it did, I would stop, because boxing, of all sports, deserves to be written about with passion and enthusiasm.

The sport has brought me many rewarding friendships, some with fellow-hacks like Bob Mee, Mike Gillender, Graham Houston and John Rawling, and others with former fighters like Billy Aird and Gary Davidson. Gary used to be the office boy at *Boxing News*, and later became a fine professional bantamweight whose career was wrecked by recurring cuts. But at least he won the Southern Area title, and I had the honour of presenting him with the championship belt in the Albert Hall ring.

Gary is now in the final stages of motor neurone disease, able to communicate only by operating a keyboard with his neck muscles, but his humour is as bright as ever. His uncomplaining bravery and total lack of self-pity set an inspiring example to us all. I dedicate this book to him with a degree of affection and respect he would be embarrassed to acknowledge.

Harry Mullan, Bridge, Kent, 1997

Opposite: Muhammed Ali defeats Joe Frazier over 12 thrilling rounds in New York in 1974.

THE POWER BROKERS

BOXING exists in a state of near-anarchy, the only major sport which does not have a single, worldwide regulatory body. Instead, there are five widely accepted organizations, each with its own champions and ratings lists, and at least as many again seeking recognition. At national level the sport is generally well run, but chaos reigns on the world scene as the game's credibility is destroyed.

The Organizations

BY ITS very nature, professional boxing does not lend itself to organization. It is the most individualistic of sports, and therefore the most anarchic. Tennis, soccer, athletics – every other major sport has a central, controlling body that regulates championships and imposes discipline and codes of conduct, but boxing thrives on chaos. Yet to the uninitiated, the game looks like regulating itself to death with, at last count, five widely accepted 'world governing bodies' and at least as many again lurking in the wings.

Peel away the initials, though, and you will find that, generally speaking, the real power lies with the promoters who stage the championships of the organization concerned, and on whom the organization depends for existence through the sanctioning fees the promoter pays it for the privilege of staging its contests. The bureaucrats who administer the multifarious sets of initials may well be honest and hard-working individuals, who truly believe they are acting in the best interests of the sport they serve, but with a few exceptions they are little more than puppets and mouthpieces for the money men.

At national level, matters are better: the British Boxing Board of Control, for example, does a good job of administering the business in this country, and their counterparts in the other member countries of the European Boxing Union are for the most part equally competent. But then there is a vast difference between the revenue generated by British or European championships and the multi-millions that world title fights bring in. The proliferation of would-be world governing bodies over the last twenty years is explained by a simple equation: more organizations = more titles = more (relatively) cheap audience pullers for the ever-expanding number of TV stations = more money for everyone in the game.

The purists don't like it, but the days of only eight weight divisions and just one title-holder in each division belong to the game's history as much as twenty-round title fights, or bare-knuckle fights to a finish on river barges. Championship boxing today cannot exist without television funding, and the television networks don't much care which set of initials adorn their Saturday night Big Fight so long as the viewers switch on and the advertisers pay up.

Because television companies on both sides of the Atlantic tend to align themselves with one promoter, the chosen promoter becomes a man of substantial influence within the organization whose fights he stages. In Britain, for example, Barry Hearn and later Frank Warren have staged more World Boxing Organization (WBO) contests than anyone else, and naturally the WBO will favour their interests in matters such as nominating contenders, world ratings, defence deadlines and the like. There is nothing

Left: In the days before so-called 'governing bodies', publications like the *Police Gazette* were considered the game's voice of authority. The cover illustration of this issue shows Bob Fitzsimmons beating Jack Dempsey.

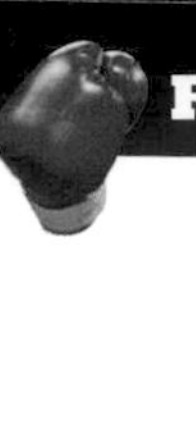

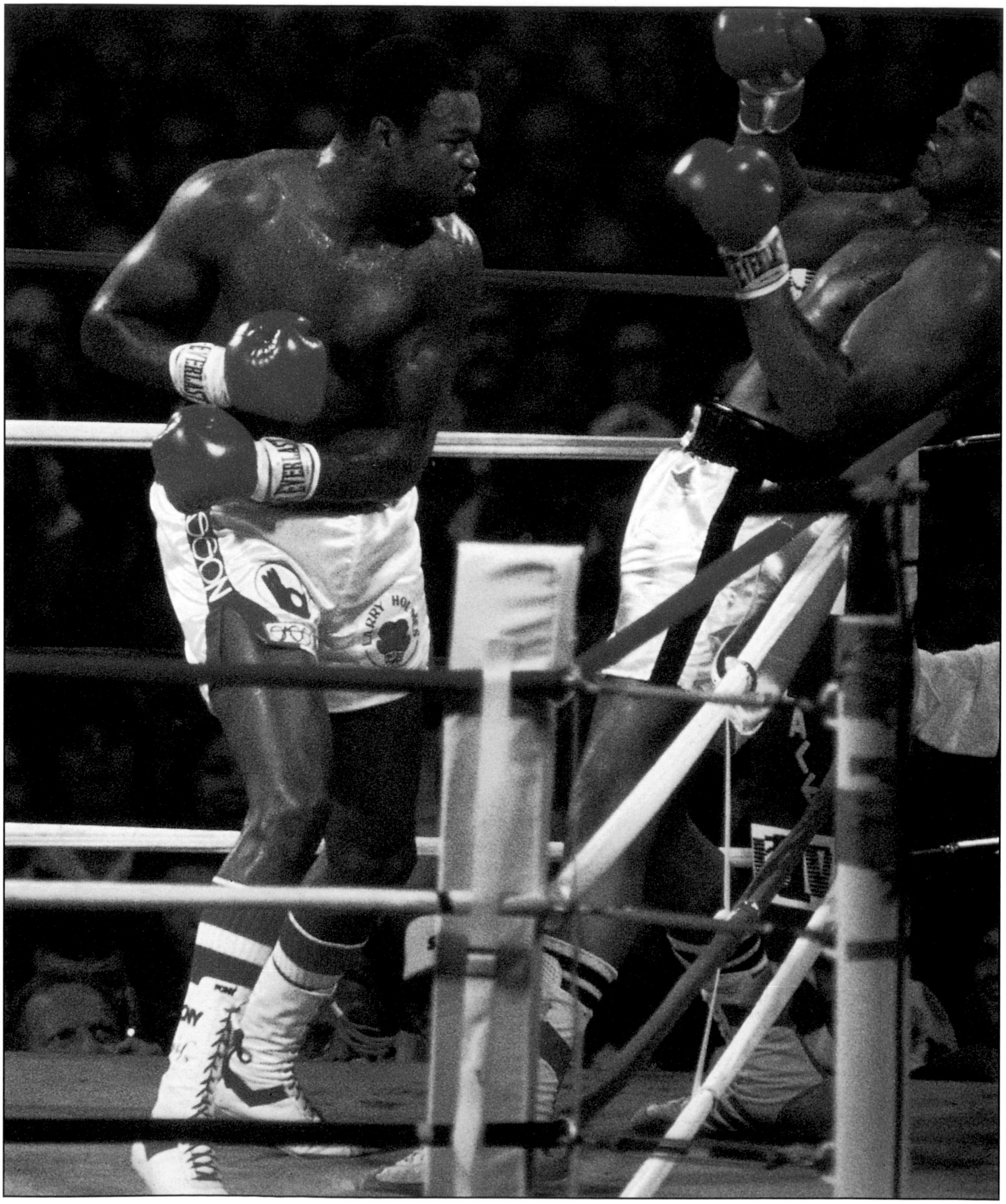
EVERLAST
EVERLAST
EVERLAST
LARRY HOLMES

mproper or corrupt in that: it is merely good business practice, because the promoter and the organization need each other.

In the days before television money became the dominant single force in boxing, life was much simpler. In the absence of any formal controlling body, the sporting press assumed a degree of power and influence that would be unthinkable today. Publications like the *Police Gazette* and later *Ring* magazine became the oracle on boxing matters: they determined the strength of rival championship claims, and when *Ring* started compiling world top ten ratings in the late 1920s their list quickly became accepted world wide as the definitive opinion.

Boxing then was centred on New York, where most of the major title fights were staged in places like Madison Square Garden, the Polo Grounds and Yankee Stadium. The New York State Athletic Commission (NYSAC), which supervised the running of the sport in the State, was therefore the single most influential administrative body in the world, and the various European national controlling bodies tended to follow New York's lead in preference to the rival National Boxing Association (NBA), which comprised (at its foundation in 1920) twenty other American States. With the explosion of television interest in boxing in the early 1960s, everything changed. The power base shifted from New York to Las Vegas, and the NYSAC was soon relegated to being precisely what its name implied – no more than a local authority.

In 1962 the NBA renamed itself the World Boxing Association (WBA), although for the next twelve years it remained strictly North American-controlled. The WBA had affiliations from 51 state commissions, many of which rarely if ever hosted boxing shows. The WBA began issuing its own ratings and imposing edicts on the existing world champions, and if they did not comply the WBA declared their title vacant and matched its own contenders for the championship. Thus, by the mid-1960s virtually every world title was split, and the seeds of today's anarchy were sown. There has not been a fight for the undisputed flyweight championship since April 1965, for the featherweight title since October 1967, for the light-welterweight championship since November 1967, and the story is much the same in the other divisions.

In 1974 two Panamanians, Gilberto Mendoza and Elias Cordoba, staged a brilliantly planned coup that removed the WBA from American hands and made it a Latin body, which it remains. However, that did not stop American promoters from staging fights under WBA auspices, and the most successful of these was Bob Arum, who worked almost exclusively with the WBA in the 1980s when he was promoting stars such as Marvin Hagler, Thomas Hearns, Mike McCallum and Ray Mancini. Arum, ever the pragmatist, had no qualms about paying hefty bribes to the WBA via a 'bag man', Pepe Cordero. According to interviews Arum gave to *Sports Illustrated* and *Ring*, he routinely gave five-figure amounts to Cordero in return for his help in 'fixing' matters with the WBA. Arum's interviews prompted some serious house-cleaning at the WBA, and its reputation improved with the introduction of South African officials (the WBA was the only boxing organization to offer South Africa membership during the apartheid era).

In 1983 Robert Lee of the New Jersey SAC led an attempted coup at the WBA convention, hoping to restore it to American control, and when this failed Lee and his friends walked out to start their own organization, the International Boxing Federation (IBF). They were backed by major American

Left: Larry Holmes (here beating Ali) was without doubt the world's best heavyweight for years, but politics denied him the undisputed title.

Right: Mike Tyson, the last man to unify the heavyweight championship.

omoters like Arum and the Duva family, and were given a major boost when star champions like heavyweight Larry Holmes and light-welterweight Aaron Pryor relinquished their other belts to accept recognition from the new body. The IBF also drew strong support from the Orient, where television input had made boxing a leading and very lucrative sport. They had a brief period of success in Britain, where Terry Marsh, Duke McKenzie, Lloyd Honeyghan, Glenn McCrory and Dave McAuley all held IBF titles in the 1980s. But the organization over-reached itself when it tried to set up the IBF-UK as a rival to the British Boxing Board of Control, and no IBF title fight has been held in Britain since 1994.

Left: Hearns and Ray Leonard, who unified the welterweight title in 1981, fought a draw in this rematch for the WBC super-middleweight title eight years later.

The WBO was another breakaway from the WBA, this time led by their former bribes-collector Pepe Cordero of Puerto Rico. The new organization took a long time to find any significant measure of acceptance in America, but Barry Hearn and then Frank Warren worked with it eagerly from the start so that Britain was soon the WBO's major power-base. Administratively, the WBO has benefited from the reshuffle forced upon it by the death of Cordero in 1995 and the departure of its President, Ed Levine, to the newly established World Boxing Union (WBU). It has had some top-quality champions like Oscar De La Hoya, Marco Antonio Barrera, Chris Eubank, Steve Collins, Naseem Hamed and Riddick Bowe, and as the IBF's power recedes the WBO is gaining strength.

The WBU, the latest candidate for membership of the inner circle of controlling bodies, was founded by Jon Robinson, a Londoner and once the IBF's European representative who, in that capacity, tried and failed to set up the IBF-UK. Robinson eventually left the IBF and moved to a Norfolk village which, bizarrely, is now the headquarters of an organization that has made rapid strides in its short life. The WBU's champions, past and present, include George Foreman, Thomas Hearns, James Toney and Montell Griffin. The WBU has recently staged its first championship fight in Britain, when Shea Neary from Liverpool won the light-welterweight title.

While all these other bodies were forming and fragmenting, the most reputable of all the organizations consolidated its position at the head of the field. The World Boxing Council (WBC) was formed in Mexico City in 1963 at a meeting attended by sixteen countries, and under the ener-getic stewardship of its presi-dent since 1975, Jose Sulaiman, it has grown to the point where it now claims the allegiance of over 100 national and regional federations. The most often heard criticism of the WBC is that

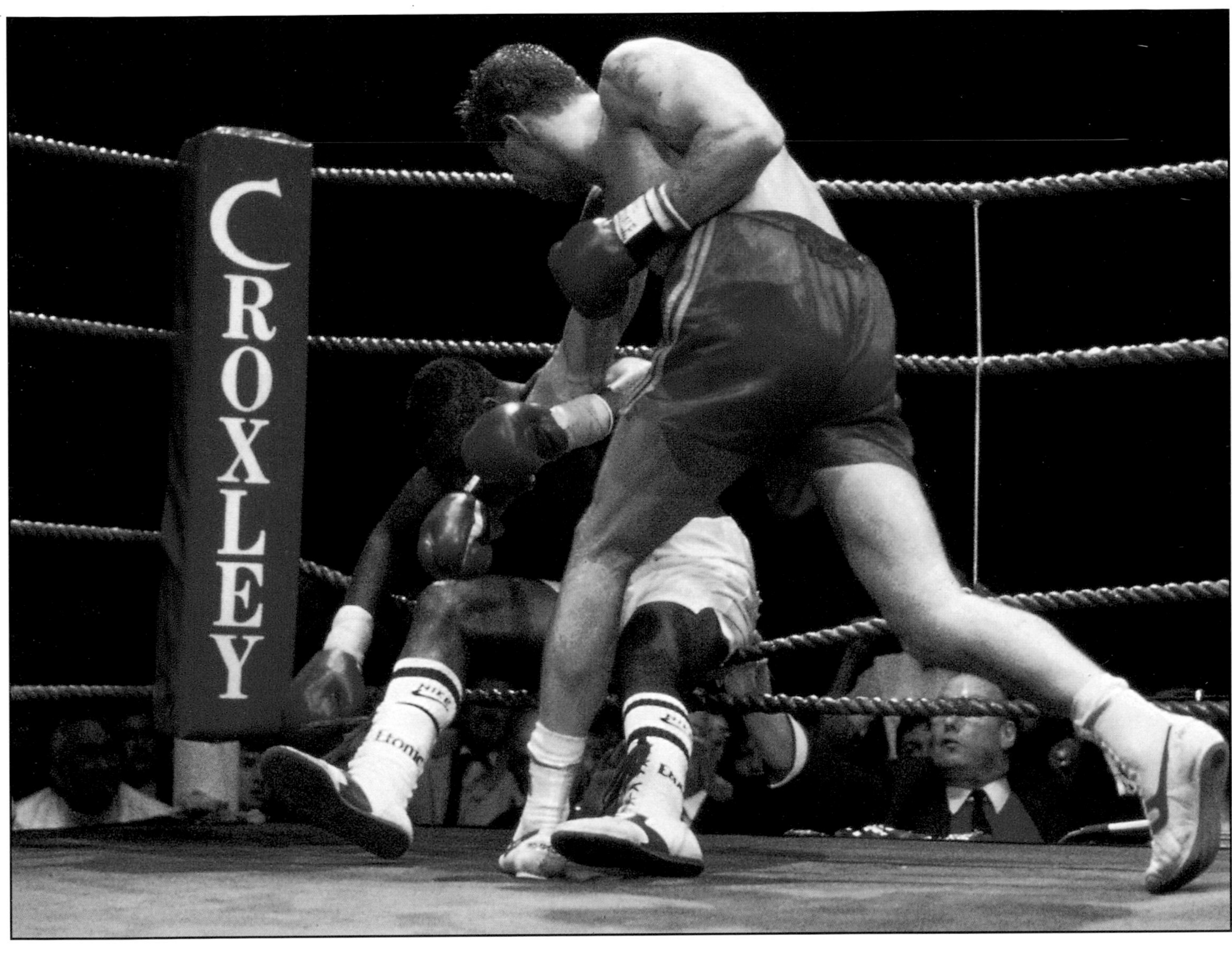

Above: McCrory punches Makhatini into the ropes and out of contention in their cruiserweight title bout.

Sulaiman is overly accommodating to Don King, who has been the organization's chief promoter (and therefore bank-roller) for the past twenty years. While this criticism is well founded, it should be said that Sulaiman has been responsible for many improvements in boxing safety, including the reduction of championships from fifteen to twelve rounds. He can appear pompous and his rhetorical style is so overblown that it jars on European ears, but there is no doubting his sincerity or the passion he feels for his sport.

There are a number of other minor outfits like the World Athletic Association, which was set up by the maverick Oklahoma promoter Pat O'Grady as a vehicle for his son Sean (formerly the WBA lightweight champion) and son-in-law Monte Masters, whom O'Grady installed as 'world heavyweight champion'. But O'Grady's enthusiasm for the project soon withered when Sean lost the lightweight title in his first defence to Andy Ganigan, while Masters split from his wife and was promptly stripped of his championship belt.

The International Boxing Organization (IBO) is gaining a foothold in Denmark, where local promoter Mogens Palle works on the long-established principle that the fans could not care less about initials so long as they are given title fights. Palle has worked with virtually all the Alphabet Boys at one time or another but is currently the only European to stage IBO championships, although British welterweight champion Kevin Lueshing won the IBO title in New York in 1996.

THE DEAL MAKERS

IN boxing, real power rests in the hand of a very few individuals. This small group of promoters, managers, TV executives, casino officials and administrators tend to function in the way of medieval barons, with a network of subsidiaries who serve as 'front' managers for their stables, or promote small shows under their auspices to give their boxers steady work. A few, like Don King, Frank Warren, Lou Duva and Bob Arum, are known to every fan, but there are other powerful figures who are content to stay in the background and make their deals: men like Rich Rose.

Rich Rose

Only the fight game's insiders know him, yet Rose commands the kind of multi-million dollar budget that ensures that Don King, Bob Arum and the rest always return his phone calls. Rose, 46, is President of Sports for the entire Caesar's Palace organization, including their Las Vegas, Atlantic City and Lake Tahoe operations, and that makes him a pivotal figure in the high finance world of modern professional boxing.

From his luxurious office suite on the 26th floor of Century Park West near Los Angeles airport, Rose negotiates the vast range of sporting attractions staged at Caesars to draw the punters to the gaming tables, but boxing is his first love. Unlike most executive types, Rose worked first in the PR business and developed an easy relationship with the press, a familiarity he uses to full advantage in his present role. He is on first-name terms with all the international reporters who regularly cover fights at Caesar's, and the range of press services and facilities he provides is unmatched.

His experience puts him above the political in-fighting that afflicts the sport, and means that he can deal with parties who won't even talk to each other. 'That's important when you're trying to make a particularly attractive fight,' he says. He has achieved the near-impossible by having King and Arum stage co-promotions there, including the Julio Cesar Chavez versus Oscar De La Hoya fight in June 1996.

Boxing draws gamblers to the machines and the tables, and it is no accident that you have to walk through the casino to get to the arena. Without casino money, many of boxing's classic fights could not have been made; without the huge injection of money a big fight means for the whole Las Vegas economy, the casinos would suffer. It's a happy marriage, and men like Rich Rose make it work.

Don King

But while Rose is self-effacing, Don King is all noise and bluster, a shock-haired, garrulous huckster and hustler who hasn't stopped for breath since he first exploded onto the boxing scene after his release from a four-year manslaughter term in 1971. King talked his way into Muhammad Ali's trust, and prised the champion away

Bob Arum, lawyer turned big-time boxing promoter.

The volatile Lou Duva always makes himself heard.

The King of the deal-makers, in full flow.

The WBC's long-serving President Jose Sulaiman.

from his previous involvement with Bob Arum. Using Ali as his power base, King expanded into management and signed up most of the leading contenders, so that when Ali retired and the title fragmented King was ideally placed to snap up the various versions and, by matching his own boxers for them, make sure that they remained under his control.

It was a brilliant strategy, ruthlessly executed, and within a decade of leaving jail the former numbers racketeer was the single most important man in boxing. He was not just a superb wheeler-dealer, but also a promoter of genius. The Las Vegas casinos were happy to work with him because they knew he could deliver the kind of shows that brought dollar-laden punters into their gambling halls. When Evander Holyfield broke his stranglehold on the heavyweight division, King switched his attention to the lighter weights and made superstars out of men like Julio Cesar Chavez, Julian

Mickey Duff dominated British boxing for over 20 years.

Frank Warren, now Britain's No. 1 promoter.

Jackson, Terry Norris and Azumah Nelson, and was thus able to maintain his position at the forefront of the business when Mike Tyson (whom he had 'acquired' in 1988) was jailed.

While Tyson was inside, King rebuilt his heavyweight empire so that when the former champion was released, King was the only man in a position to plot his route back to the title. Tyson's post-prison fights grossed him anywhere between $60m and $100m: what they grossed for King can only be guessed at.

Frank Warren

King has built a solid international operation, one to which British promoter Frank Warren is central. Warren, an urbane man in his early forties who is also a free-spending patron of the arts, grabbed the complacent world of British boxing by the throat in the early 1980s and shook it until it squealed. A former promoter of unlicensed shows, he was persuaded to come into the fold and promptly challenged decades of convention and custom, forcing the Board to back down repeatedly and make the sport a more open and competitive business. When Warren emerged in the early 1980s, Mickey Duff and his associates enjoyed a virtual monopoly of television coverage on BBC, and since there was no rival promoter to compete, ITV had dropped out of the sport. Warren enticed them back, using the unlikely figure of Joe Bugner – on yet another comeback – as the lure.

He established a profitable and successful liaison with ITV, gradually edging Duff to the sidelines until the wheel came full circle and BBC pulled out because their promoter was no longer able to supply the names the public wanted to watch. Warren survived a shooting and a catastrophic business slump to claw his way back to the top of British boxing, and in 1995 made a multi-million pound deal with Sky Sports, who bought exclusive rights to his ever-expanding stable of champions.

The deal left Warren clear of the field in Britain with Duff – once the unchallenged No. 1 – seemingly content to wind down his operation and concentrate on management, and Barry Hearn, who once looked like becoming his chief rival, spending 1996 in a process of rebuilding and regrouping after the departure of major stars like Chris Eubank, Herbie Hide and Nigel Benn. Of the rest, only the irrepressible Frank Maloney, a former small-time matchmaker and promoter who confounded the establishment by securing Lennox Lewis's contract, has the potential to give Warren a run for his money.

Maloney and his backer, Panos Eliades, have done a first-rate job of managing Lewis and the WBC champion has remained commendably loyal to them despite Don King's best efforts to tempt him away. Maloney has built up a useful stable of young fighters who, like the British super-featherweight champion P. J. Gallagher, are poised to move on to a bigger stage when the inevitable happens and Lewis departs.

Frank Maloney - from small time to major league.

The late Dan Duva, of the Main Events company.

Bob Arum

In America, Bob Arum remains Don King's main rival. A former tax lawyer who became interested in boxing while investigating the financial structure of he Patterson vs. Liston heavyweight title fight in 1962, he is very much a businessman rather than a showman and his personality is the antithesis of King's. But his business-like approach impressed top names like Muhammad Ali, Marvin Hagler, Sugar Ray Leonard, Don Curry, Roberto Duran, Hector Camacho and James Toney, all of whom were promoted regularly by Arum. Hagler stayed with him throughout his long championship career, and it was through him that Arum's close links with Caesars Palace were forged.

Oscar De La Hoya is currently Arum's major drawing card, which should ensure that Arum remains in the top bracket for many years. He has ensured a steady supply of young talent through his regular promotions on the ESPN network in America, which stages small televised shows across the country.

Cedric Kushner

Television is also the key to success for Cedric Kushner, an affable, generously waisted South African who made his fortune in promoting rock concerts after working his way to America on a cargo boat. Kushner is closely involved with the IBF, and stages many of their title fights around the world in association with local promoters, as well as running frequent televised shows in America, mainly in New York and Las Vegas.

The Duva Family

The other main operator in America is an organization called Main Events, the New Jersey promotional company belonging to the Duva family. Lou Duva, the head of the operation, is a trainer and manager of the old school whose fierce commitment to his boxers has led to his involvement in some spectacular brawls in the ring.

He worked his way up the ranks, starting as a preliminary fighter himself, to learn the business at all levels. His son Dan was groomed to run the business side of the operation while Lou concentrated on developing the talent, which he did brilliantly with fighters such as Evander Holyfield, John-John Molina, Meldrick Taylor, Mike McCallum and Pernell Whitaker.

The family's first big-time promotion was the Sugar Ray Leonard vs. Thomas Hearns welterweight unification match in 1981, and they were responsible for many subsequent classics throughout the 1980s and 1990s.

The family was sorely hit by the early death of Dan, aged 44, in January 1996 but the business goes on with another son, Dino, at the helm.

Chapter 1

Modern Greats

EVERY generation produces a handful of fighters who will be remembered with reverence long after their careers are over. Some of those we look at here, men like Marvin Hagler, Alexis Arguello or Roberto Duran, had primes that spanned a decade or longer. Others, like the ill-fated Aaron Pryor, rose and fell like a rocket but illuminated the sport during their brief spell at the top. Either way, their place with the game's legends is secure.

R O U N D

First dent in the armour – Julio Cesar Chavez (right) is held to a draw by Pernell Whitaker in their WBC welterweight title fight. After 87 straight wins, it is the end of the Mexican's perfect record.

MODERN GREATS

ALEXIS ARGUELLO

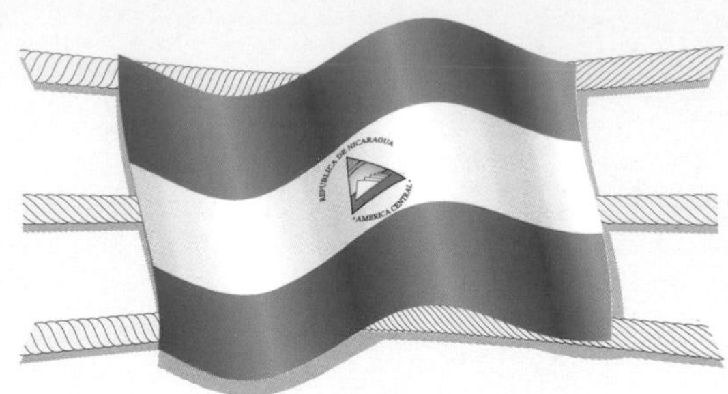

ALEXIS ARGUELLO was made for television. The handsome, moustachioed Nicaraguan looked like a film star, had the personality of a presidential candidate and fought like a demon to win three world titles and become a superstar in the 1970s and early 1980s. He started as a pencil-slim 16-year-old featherweight in 1968, and a loss in his first pro fight stilled any hopes of instant glory. But by 1973 he was becoming a force in the division, and a first-round knockout of former champion Jose Legra earned him a crack at Ernesto Marcel's WBA title in 1974. Marcel won on points but the experience was invaluable to the youngster and before the year was out he had KO'd Marcel's successor Ruben Olivares to become champion.

After four defences he relinquished the title to move up to super-featherweight, where he won the WBC title in 1978. He proved one of that division's best champions, making eight successful defences against top men like Bobby Chacon, Alfredo Escalera, Rafael Limon and Ruben Castillo. By late 1980 he could no longer make the weight, and gave up that title to challenge Scotland's Jim Watt for the WBC lightweight title at Wembley. It was Britain's only glimpse of Arguello in action, and he gave a vintage performance to send the Scot into retirement with a points win. Watt was floored in the seventh but rallied stubbornly to last the full 15 rounds.

Arguello made four defences, including a 14th-round defeat of TV favourite Ray Mancini on an emotion-charged night when Mancini tried to win the title for his father, Lennie, who had been a championship contender until the Second World War ended his career. Arguello won brilliantly, and the dignity and sensitivity he showed afterwards to Mancini senior (who watched the fight from a ringside wheelchair) and his beaten opponent endeared him to the American public (Mancini later won the WBA version of the title).

In 1982 Arguello tried for a fourth title when he stood head-to-head with the unstoppable Aaron Pryor for fourteen rounds in a classic clash for the WBA light-welterweight title, a fight in which Arguello absorbed dreadful punishment. The rematch in 1983 also ended in defeat, this time in ten rounds, and thereafter Arguello boxed only sporadically, retiring in 1986. He lost most of his money in the Nicaraguan Civil War and made a brief two-fight comeback in 1994–5, before retiring for good in 1995 with a record of only eight defeats in 88 fights.

The change of government in Nicaragua after the defeat of the Sandanistas meant a change of luck for Arguello, whose claims for compensation for the cash and property confiscated by the previous government were sympathetically received. Enough was restored to him to render a further comeback unnecessary.

FORM LINE

Born:	**19 April 1952, Managua, Nicaragua**
Height:	**5ft 10 in**
Weight:	**122–142 lb**
Pro debut:	**1 August 1968, Managua; Cachorro Amaya, lost, ref stopped fight Round 1**
Last fight:	**21 January 1995, Las Vegas; Scott Walker, lost on pts, 10 rounds**
Total fights:	**88**
Wins:	**80 (64 inside schedule)**
Losses:	**8 (4 inside schedule)**
Champ. record:	**19 wins, 3 defeats**
Titles:	**WBA featherweight champion, 1974–7; WBC super-featherweight champion, 1978–81; WBC lightweight champion, 1981–3**

Britain saw the handsome Arguello at his best when he came to Wembley in 1981 to end Jim Watt's reign as WBC lightweight champion. It was the Scot's last fight, and victory made the Nicaraguan a three-time world champion.

JULIO CESAR CHAVEZ

THE ACID test of legendary status is whether a once-great fighter's aura survives even when he is in decline. Roberto Duran's does, and so, unmistakably, does that which surrounds Mexican idol Julio Cesar Chavez. Oscar De La Hoya dazzled him to defeat in June 1996 to take the last of his three world titles, but Chavez's popularity remains undiminished as, like Duran, he chases the 100th win which he promises will close a fabulous career dating back to February 1980. For a long time it looked as though he might even make 100 fights without a loss, but defeat finally came in his 91st contest in thirteen years when Frankie Randall took his WBC light-welterweight crown.

Chavez won his first championship in his 44th fight, stopping Mario Martinez for the vacant WBC super-featherweight title. It was his 38th quick win, and he retained the title nine times before moving up to lightweight in 1987 to take the WBA belt from Edwin Rosario and the WBC championship from Jose Luis Ramirez a year later. In 1989, he took the WBC light-welterweight title from Roger Mayweather and then scored one of the most famous victories in ring history when, trailing hopelessly on points, he mounted one last attack which crushed IBF champion Meldrick Taylor with just two seconds left in the final round.

He retained the 10-stone title eight times, then moved up again for an ambitious challenge for Pernell Whitaker's WBC welterweight title. The sleek American looked to have won their San Antonio twelve-rounder clearly but the judges, perhaps influenced by the strong Mexican contingent in the crowd, scored the fight a draw. The slide continued as he lost to Randall, but he regained the title in a rematch and made a further four defences before losing in four rounds to De La Hoya.

With De La Hoya set to relinquish the light-welterweight title to challenge for Pernell Whitaker's welterweight title in April 1997, the legendary Mexican might yet pull off one last, late-career success by taking the vacant title again. Whatever happens, though, his place with the sport's greats is secure.

Chavez at his best was almost robotic, a methodical stylist who never appeared ruffled or hurried but whose short hooks and crippling body punches took the fight out of a whole generation of lightweight and light-welterweight stars. He has achieved the kind of status in Mexico which Pele enjoys in Brazil, and only his lack of adequate English has prevented him from becoming a truly international superstar. But for those who know their boxing, he is the greatest Mexican fighter of all time and that is a considerable accolade.

Above: The Pride of Mexico salutes yet another triumph in a glittering career.

FORM LINE

Born:	**12 July 1962, Ciudad Obregon, Sonora, Mexico**
Height:	**5ft 7 in**
Weight:	**127–145 lb**
Pro debut:	**5 February1980, Culiacan; Andres Felix, won, KO Round 6**
Last fight:	**12 October 1996, Anaheim; Joey Gamache, won, ref stopped fight Round 8**
Total fights:	**100**
Wins:	**97 (82 inside schedule)**
Losses:	**2 (1 inside schedule)**
Champ. record:	**31 wins, 3 defeats**
Titles:	**WBC super-featherweight champion 1984–7; WBA lightweight champion 1987–8; WBC lightweight champion 1988–9; WBC light-welterweight champion 1989–94, 1995–6; IBF light-welterweight champion 1990–1**

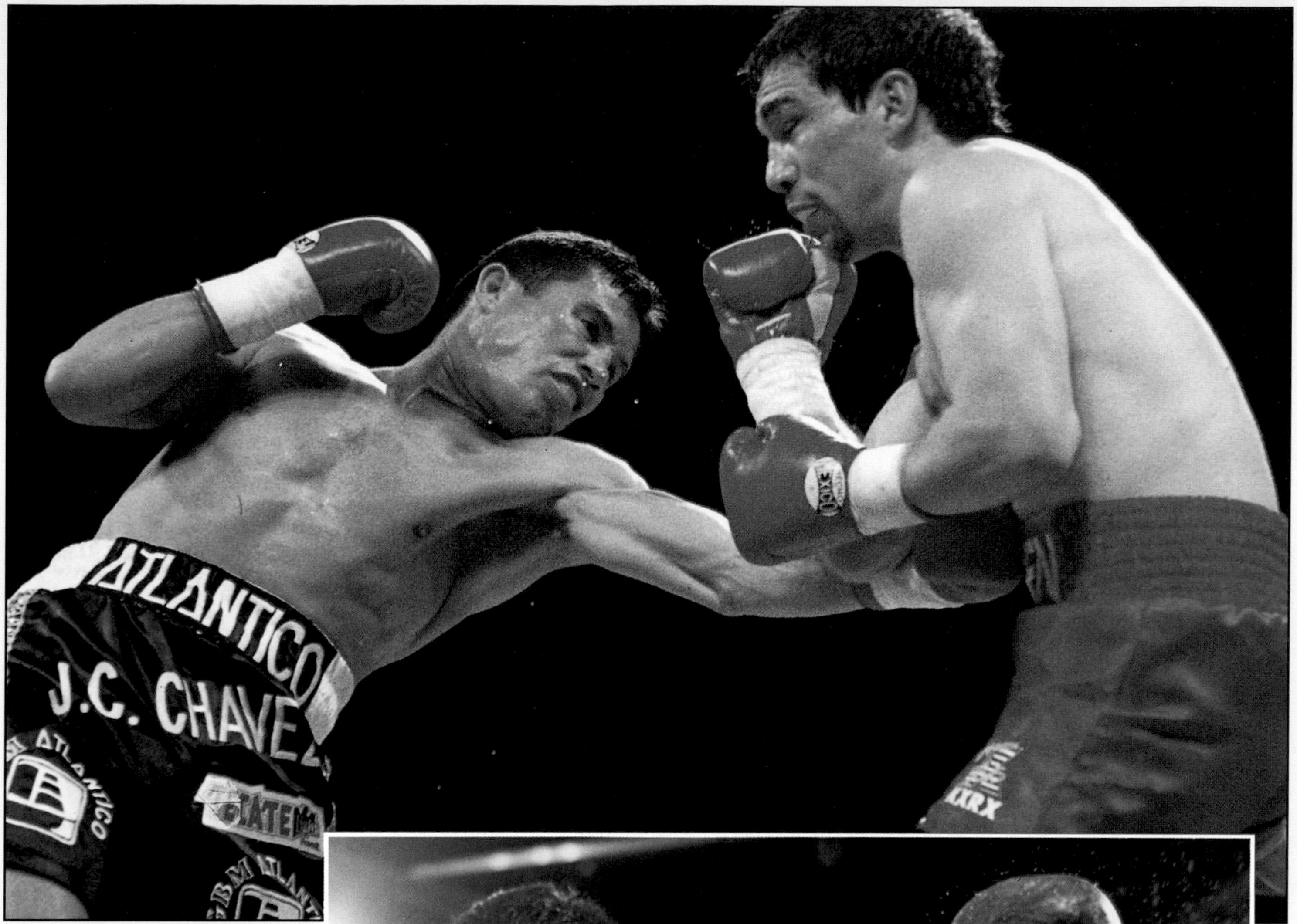

Above: Chavez lands an inch-perfect left to the body against rugged Greg Haugen in their 1993 clash for the WBC light-welter title, which Chavez won in five rounds.

Right: Chavez had a desperate struggle with Meldrick Taylor in their first fight, but handled the American easily in their 1994 rematch in Las Vegas.

MODERN GREATS

ROBERTO DURAN

ROBERTO DURAN, for many the finest fighter of his generation, once said 'There's no boxer in the world who doesn't fight for money' – but has spent years contradicting himself by boxing for the sheer enjoyment the sport gives him. As this was written late in 1996, the indefatigable Panamanian was one short of 100 victories in a professional career that began in March 1967, before most of his recent opponents were even born. He first appeared in the world ratings in 1969 and has rarely been out of them since, an astonishing achievement considering that he has boxed at world championship level from lightweight (9 st 9 lb) to super-middleweight (12 st).

He was raised in Chorillo, a disease-infested slum on the east side of the Panama Canal. His father deserted the family, leaving Roberto to help his mother raise her nine children alone. The ring provided an escape route, and he turned pro at the age of fifteen after winning thirteen of his sixteen amateur fights. His natural ferocity brought him 21 wins in a row (sixteen by knockout) and attracted local millionaire Carlos Eleta, who bought his contract for $300. Ironically, as a boy Duran used to climb the walls around Eleta's orchard to steal fruit, a debt that was more than repaid when he won the WBA lightweight title from Scotland's Ken Buchanan ten days after his 21st birthday. He went on to make twelve defences, equalling the all-time record, and unified the championship in the last of these by knocking out WBC champ Esteban DeJesus, the only man to have beaten him in 64 fights.

Plagued by weight problems, he moved up to welterweight, where he won the WBC title from Sugar Ray Leonard in June 1980. It was a famous victory, yet he quit abruptly in the rematch three months later with the immortal words 'No mas, no mas' ('No more, no more'). His action – never satisfactorily explained – destroyed his reputation, but he redeemed himself by winning the WBA light-middleweight title on his 32nd birthday and then defying mighty Marvin Hagler for fifteen rounds in a bid for the middleweight title. In 1989, he scored a shock points win over Iran Barkley to take the WBC middleweight title, and although it was his last championship success he has continued to compete at top level, winning more than he loses.

Some of his recent defeats have been close enough for argument, including a pair of controversial fights with Vinny Pazienza and a razor-thin loss to Hector Camacho. Had those gone his way, the astonishing Panamanian could have entered his 30th professional year still a world title contender. Instead, he fights on into 1997 because of a huge unpaid tax bill from the Panamanian government – shades of Joe Louis, another legend laid low by the taxman.

Above: The original Macho Man, still going strong at the age of 46.

FORM LINE

Born:	**16 June 1951, Gurare, Panama**
Height:	**5 ft 7 in**
Weight:	**114–171 lb**
Pro debut:	**8 March 1967, Panama City; Carlos Mendoza, won on pts**
Last fight:	**15 February 1997, Mar Del Plata, Argentina; Jorge Castro lost on pts, 10 rounds**
Total fights:	**112**
Wins:	**99 (69 inside schedule)**
Losses:	**13 (3 inside schedule)**
Champ. record:	**31 wins, 3 defeats**
Titles:	**WBA lightweight champion, 1972–8, world lightweight champion, 1978–9, WBC welterweight champion, 1980; WBA light-middleweight champion, 1983–4, WBC middleweight champion, 1989–90**

Right: Roberto can still handle the youngsters: here, he stops Roni Martinez in seven rounds in 1995. While some would have retired into comparative, but wealthy, obscurity, Duran is forced to remain in the ring by the sheer size of the tax bill the Panamanian government has levied against him.

Below: Robbie Sims, Marvin Hagler's half-brother, completes a family double over Duran by outpointing him in 1986. While he still competes at the highest levels, he has not won a championship since 1989, when he beat Iran Barkley for the WBC Middleweight belt.

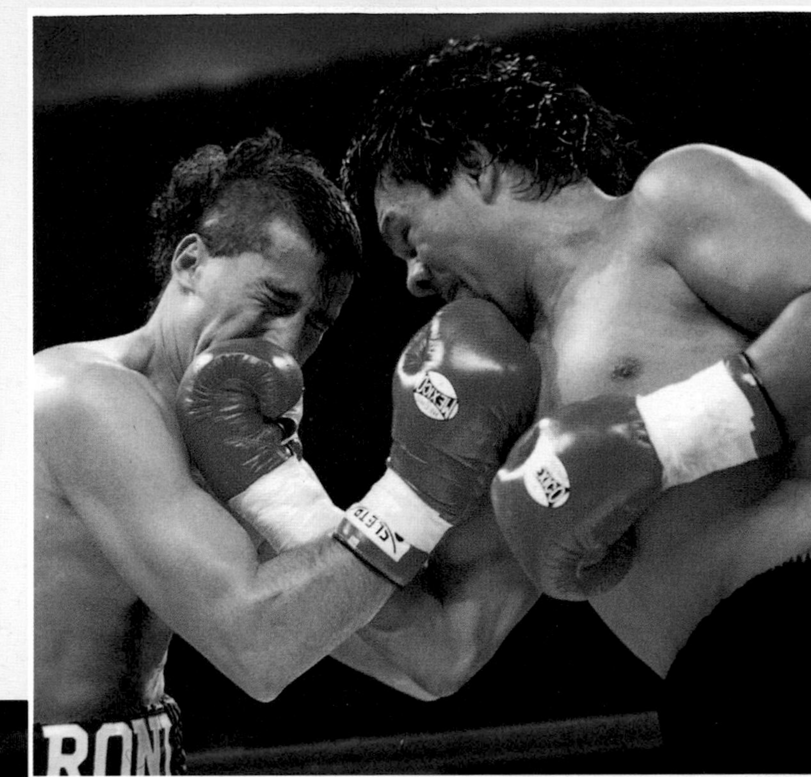

MARVIN HAGLER

SHAVEN-SKULLED and menacing, Marvin Hagler dominated the middleweight division for a decade. He would have reigned for even longer had boxing politics not denied him an earlier opportunity to become champion, and then a bitterly disputed verdict cost him his title against Sugar Ray Leonard in 1987. Hagler walked away from the game after that, and resisted all attempts to lure him back. That alone made him something of a rarity: staying retired, as too many once-great champions have learned to their cost, is not easy, yet Hagler was strong enough to quit at the top and keep his reputation intact.

And what a reputation it was. He earned it the hard way, working up through the ranks without a well-connected promoter to back him or a sympathetic TV network to bankroll his fights. Joe Frazier was an early admirer of the youngster, who turned professional after winning the 1973 AAU middleweight title. 'You've got three strikes against you', he warned Hagler. 'You're good, you're a southpaw and you're black.' Marvin stayed loyal to the Petronelli brothers, Goody and Pat, who had taught him his amateur skills in their gym in Brockton, the Massachusetts town to which Hagler's mother had moved her family after the race riots in their home city of Newark, New Jersey in 1967.

The partnership endured, and the Petronellis trained and managed Marvin to the end of his career. Once he reached contender status, a laborious process that took him 50 fights of which he lost just two, Bob Arum's Top Rank organization promoted his fights and staged most of his championship contests. He was finally given a crack at the title in 1979, but champion Vito Antuofermo held him to a disputed draw in Las Vegas. In 1980 Hagler took the title from Britain's Alan Minter, and went on to retain it twelve times, including epic victories over Thomas Hearns and John Mugabi, whom he stopped in thrilling battles at Caesars Palace, Las Vegas. He seemed indestructible, able to absorb the hardest punches without apparent effect and blessed with an enviable ability to box equally smoothly from a southpaw or orthodox stance. Ultimately, it took a fiercely controversial verdict in Leonard's favour to end his career. In 67 fights he was beaten just three times and held to a draw twice. After his retirement he settled in Milan, where he has made a successful second career as a film actor.

FORM LINE

Born:	**23 May 1954, Newark, New Jersey**
Height:	**5ft 9½ in**
Weight:	**155–162 lb**
Pro debut:	**18 May 1973, Brockton; Terry Ryan, won, KO Round 2**
Last fight:	**6 April 1987, Las Vegas; Ray Leonard, lost on pts, 12 rounds**
Total fights:	**67**
Wins:	**62 (52 inside schedule)**
Losses:	**3**
Draws:	**2**
Champ. record:	**13 wins, 1 defeat, 1 draw**
Titles:	**World middleweight champion, 1980–6; WBC middleweight champion, 1986–7**

Left: He added the 'Marvelous' to his name by deed poll, but the adjective was accurate.

Right: Hagler looked to have beaten Ray Leonard in his final fight, but the Las Vegas judges thought not.

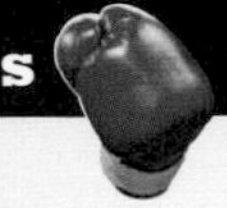

MODERN GREATS

THOMAS HEARNS

THERE WAS a measure of justice about the fact that Thomas Hearns became boxing's first five-weights world champion just three days before his great rival Sugar Ray Leonard did the same. Hearns had chased a rematch with Leonard for eight years after their epic clash for the undisputed welterweight title in 1981, and spent long periods of his career in Leonard's shadow. When they finally met again, for Leonard's WBC super-middleweight title in 1989, most observers felt Hearns was robbed by the draw verdict, but the fact that he had beaten Leonard to that record fifth championship was some consolation.

Hearns, the best-known product of Emanuel Steward's famous Kronk gym in Detroit, was the most spectacular puncher of his day, yet as an amateur international he was a light-punching, awkward boxer. Steward spotted his potential and developed it, working on Hearns' punching until the the lanky youngster was an instinctive knockout hitter with either hand. Hearns turned pro in November 1977 and was an instant sensation, racing to the WBA welterweight title in 29 fights, 27 of which ended inside the distance.

The way he dispatched the fearsome champion Pipino Cuevas of Mexico (himself an explosive puncher) in just two rounds marked him as a legend in the making. He retained the title three times before facing WBC champion Leonard in a unification match in Las Vegas in 1981, and was leading on points after thirteen rounds when Leonard, one eye closed, floored him in the 14th to force a stoppage.

Hearns moved up to take the WBC light-middleweight title from Wilfred Benitez, and his four successful defences included a crushing second-round knockout of Roberto Duran. He figured in arguably the greatest fight in history when he challenged Marvin Hagler for the middleweight title, losing in three unforgettable rounds. In 1987 he took the WBC light-heavyweight title from Dennis Andries, and won the vacant WBC middleweight title later that year before completing his championship five-timer by winning the WBO super-middleweight title in 1988.

If the claims of the recently formed World Boxing Union are recognized, Hearns is actually a six-weights champion: he won the fledgling organization's cruiserweight title in 1995, but has boxed only twice since then. The mixture of explosive power and vulnerability which characterized his style made him compulsively watchable: a supreme entertainer.

Above: The Hitman – Hearns was the fiercest puncher of his generation.

Right: History-maker – Hearns stalks James Kinchen on the way to a record-breaking fifth world title in 1988.

FORM LINE

Born	**18 October 1958, Memphis, Tennessee**
Height:	**6 ft 1 in**
Weight:	**145–180 lb**
Pro debut:	**25 November 1977, Detroit; Jerome Hill, won, KO, Round 2**
Last fight:	**29 November 1996, Virginia; Carl Willis, won, ref stopped fight Round 5**
Total fights:	**61**
Wins:	**56 (44 inside schedule)**
Losses:	**4 (3 inside schedule)**
Draws:	**1**
Champ. record:	**15 wins (10 inside schedule), 4 defeats (3 inside schedule), 1 draw**
Titles:	**WBA welterweight champion, 1980–1 WBC; light-middleweight champion, 1982–6; WBC light-heavyweight champion, 1987; WBC middleweight champion, 1987–8; WBO super-middleweight champion, 1988–91; WBA light-heavyweight champion, 1991–2; WBU cruiserweight champion, 1995–7**

LARRY HOLMES

IT WAS **Larry Holmes's misfortune that his career** should span the reigns of two of the most colourful and glamorous heavyweights of all – Muhammad Ali and Mike Tyson. At his considerable best, Holmes was good enough to hold his own with, and perhaps beat, either of them, but he was never allowed to step out of their long shadows, even though he amassed a wonderful championship record of twenty wins and five defeats. His first title fight came in 1978 and his last in 1995: only a rare few can match that for longevity at the top. At 47, Holmes was still capable of beating men young enough to be his sons.

Holmes, who had a superb left jab, learned his trade as a sparring partner for all the leading heavyweights of the time, including Ali, Joe Frazier, Ken Norton and Earnie Shavers. It was a tough school, but the lessons of the sparring ring paid off when, after compiling an unbeaten run of 26, he was matched with his former employer Shavers in an eliminator for the WBC title. Holmes won on points, and went on to take the title from Norton in one of the great fights in heavyweight history. He proved a busy champion, retaining the title sixteen times. Gerry Cooney, perhaps the best of the so-called 'White Hopes', gave him a terrific fight in 1982 but lost in thirteen rounds, and his other challengers included Mike Weaver, Leon Spinks, Tim Witherspoon and James 'Bonecrusher' Smith, all sometime world champions.

In 1980 he met the sad remnants of Muhammad Ali, who was attempting an ill-advised comeback. To his credit, Holmes refused to punish the old champion and instead pleaded with him to quit until Ali's corner finally pulled him out after ten rounds.

Holmes relinquished the WBC belt in 1983 to accept recognition from the newly formed International Boxing Federation. He retained their version of the title a further three times before losing it to Mike Spinks on a controversial decision in his fourteenth fight, thus wrecking his dream of emulating Rocky Marciano's 49-fight unbeaten record. Holmes lost to Spinks in a rematch and retired. A couple of years later he was lured back to challenge Tyson, losing predictably in four rounds. He fought his way back to lose creditably in subsequent title bids against Evander Holyfield and Oliver McCall, but was still world-ranked, at 47, as 1996 ended.

He almost managed to reclaim a finger-hold on the world title in his first fight in 1997, when he travelled to Copenhagen to challenge the unbeaten Dane Brian Nielsen for the lightly regarded IBO version of the title. Holmes, conceding 16 years, boxed as well as he has done for years and looked unlucky to lose a split decision. 'The Danes can't appreciate quality when they see it,' he complained in the dressing room. But whatever the Danes think, boxing historians will have no difficulty in ranking Holmes with the greats.

FORM LINE

Born:	**3 November 1949, Cuthbert, Georgia,**
Height:	**6 ft 3 in**
Weight:	**196–246 lb**
Pro debut:	**21 March 1973, Scranton; Rodell Dupree, won on pts, 4 rounds**
Last fight:	**24 January 1997, Copenhagen ; Brian Nielsen, lost on pts, 12 rounds**
Total fights:	**71**
Wins:	**65 (42 inside schedule)**
Losses:	**6**
Champ. record:	**20 wins (14 inside schedule), 5 defeats**
Titles:	**WBC heavyweight champion, 1978–83; IBF heavyweight champion, 1984–5**

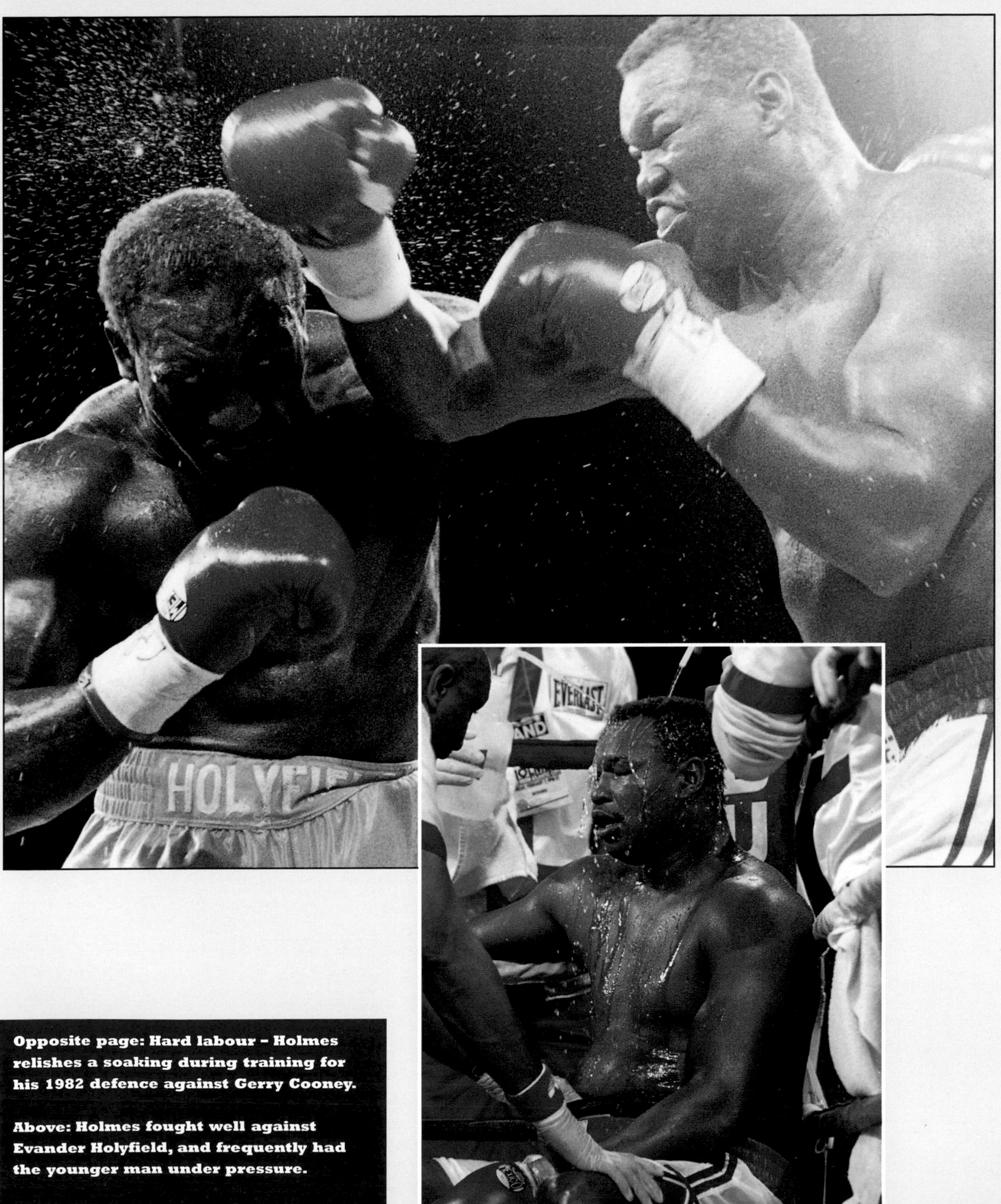

Opposite page: Hard labour – Holmes relishes a soaking during training for his 1982 defence against Gerry Cooney.

Above: Holmes fought well against Evander Holyfield, and frequently had the younger man under pressure.

Right: Middle-aged spread shows as Larry takes a breather between rounds against Ray Mercer, whom he beat on points.

MODERN GREATS

SUGAR RAY LEONARD

THROUGHOUT the 1980s the boxing world danced to Ray Leonard's tune as the game's brightest star and biggest ego dictated terms to promoters, contenders and governing bodies with equal egocentricity. He even contrived, with breathtaking arrogance, to win two titles in the same fight by compelling WBC light-heavyweight champion Donny Lalonde to scale under 12 st for a defence of the 12 st 7 lb title, so that the vacant WBC super-middleweight title could also be at stake. He manipulated the rankings and the media and even hijacked the most famous nickname in boxing history, yet such was his towering talent that he was forgiven everything. The man could fight, with a champion's heart and an iron will that would have made him a legend in any era.

Leonard lost only five out of 150 amateur contests in a dazzling career that brought him the 1976 Olympic gold medal, and made himself America's sweetheart by boxing with a photo of his young son taped to his boot. On his return from the Games, he converted that goodwill into hard cash by signing a lucrative professional contract that paid him a record purse for a pro debut and ensured that he had banked over $2m before he fought for his first title, the WBC welterweight championship, which he won from Wilfred Benitez in 1979. Arch-rival Roberto Duran took his title in a ferocious fifteen-rounder in June 1980, but Leonard learned well from the defeat, demoralizing Duran so thoroughly in the rematch that the Panamanian quit halfway through the eighth round. He unified the title by stopping WBA champion Thomas Hearns in a classic encounter (having won the WBA light-middleweight title in between), but was forced into premature retirement by a detached retina.

He made a one-fight comeback two years later, but retired again before returning for the fight he had always craved, a showdown with middleweight champion Marvin Hagler. They met at Caesars Palace in April 1987, and Leonard sneaked a split decision. After stopping Lalonde in their two-for-one title fight nineteen months later, he relinquished the light-heavyweight title and retained the super-middleweight belt twice before retiring again. He returned to action in February 1991, losing to Terry Norris for the WBC light-middleweight title, and quit again only to make a losing comeback, at 40, in 1997. Sometimes even great fighters never learn.

FORM LINE

Born:	17 May 1956, Wilmington, South Carolina
Height:	5 ft 10 in
Weight:	141–168 lb
Pro debut:	5 February 1977, Baltimore; Luis Vega, won on pts, 6 rounds
Last fight:	1 March 1997, Atlantic City; Hecto Camacho, lost, ref stopped fight Round 5
Total fights:	40
Wins:	36 (25 inside schedule)
Losses:	3
Champ. record:	10 wins (8 inside schedule), 2 defeats, 1 draw
Titles:	WBC welterweight champion, 1979–80, 1980–1; world welter-weight champion, 1981–2; WBA light-middleweight champion, 1981; WBC middleweight champion, 1987; WBC super-middleweight champion, 1988–90; WBC light-heavyweight champion, 1988

Right: Highlights from a fabulous career – taking the middleweight title from Marvin Hagler and (inset) winning Olympic gold against Andres Aldama of Cuba in 1976.

AZUMAH NELSON

THE cheery, round-faced Ghanaian known as 'The Little Professor' has no serious challenger for the title of Africa's greatest-ever boxer, and continues to prove, even in athletic old age, that he belongs with the ring's genuine superstars. He had his first world title fight in 1982, and fourteen years later was still at the summit of his profession as the WBC super-featherweight champion. Big, slow heavyweights like George Foreman can survive at the top for that kind of spell, but for a man from the lighter divisions it is remarkable.

Nelson has been a main event fighter throughout his career: his debut, on 1 December 1979, was a eight-rounder against Billy Kwame. He took the Ghanaian featherweight title in his second fight, and the All-African championship in his sixth. Trained by a veteran Liverpool coach called Charles Atkinson (whose son, Charles Jr., later turned out a host of world champions from Thailand), Nelson became Commonwealth champion in 1981. It was impressive progress, but the real breakthrough came when he was called in after only thirteen fights as a late substitute to challenge Salvador Sanchez for the WBC title in Madison Square Garden, New York. Few Americans had heard of Nelson, but his performance in taking the Mexican into the 15th round was a revelation.

He spent 1983 consolidating his position as a contender, and finally took the title from Wilfredo Gomez in December 1984. He retained it six times, all against top challengers, before moving up to super-feather where he outpointed Mario Martinez for the vacant WBC title in 1988. His nine successful defences brought him to America, England, Australia and Mexico. He challenged Pernell Whitaker for the WBC and IBF lightweight titles in 1990, but, distracted by his wife's recent death from cancer, failed to do himself justice and was clearly outpointed. In May 1994 he lost his super-featherweight title to Jesse James Leija, who had held him to a draw in a 1993 title bid, and stayed out of the ring for eighteen months. There had been no formal retirement announcement, but it was still a surprise when he announced that he was returning to challenge Leija's conqueror, Gabriel Ruelas, whom he duly stopped in December 1995. He held on to the title throughout 1996, and showed no signs of slowing up as he chased a 1997 showdown with the British star Naseem Hamed.

FORM LINE

Born:	19 July 1958, Accra, Ghana
Height:	5 ft 5 in
Weight:	124–134 lb
Pro debut:	1 December 1979, Accra; Billy Kwame, won on pts, 8 rounds
Last fight:	1 June 1996, Las Vegas; Jesse James Leija, won, ref stopped fight Round 6
Total fights:	44
Wins:	39 (28 inside schedule)
Losses:	3
Draws:	2
Champ. record:	18 wins (12 inside schedule), 3 defeats, 2 draws
Titles:	Commonwealth featherweight champion, 1981–3; WBC champion 1984–8; WBC super-featherweight champion, 1988–94, 1995

Above: The Professor acknowledges the crowd after beating Jesse James Leija in 1996.

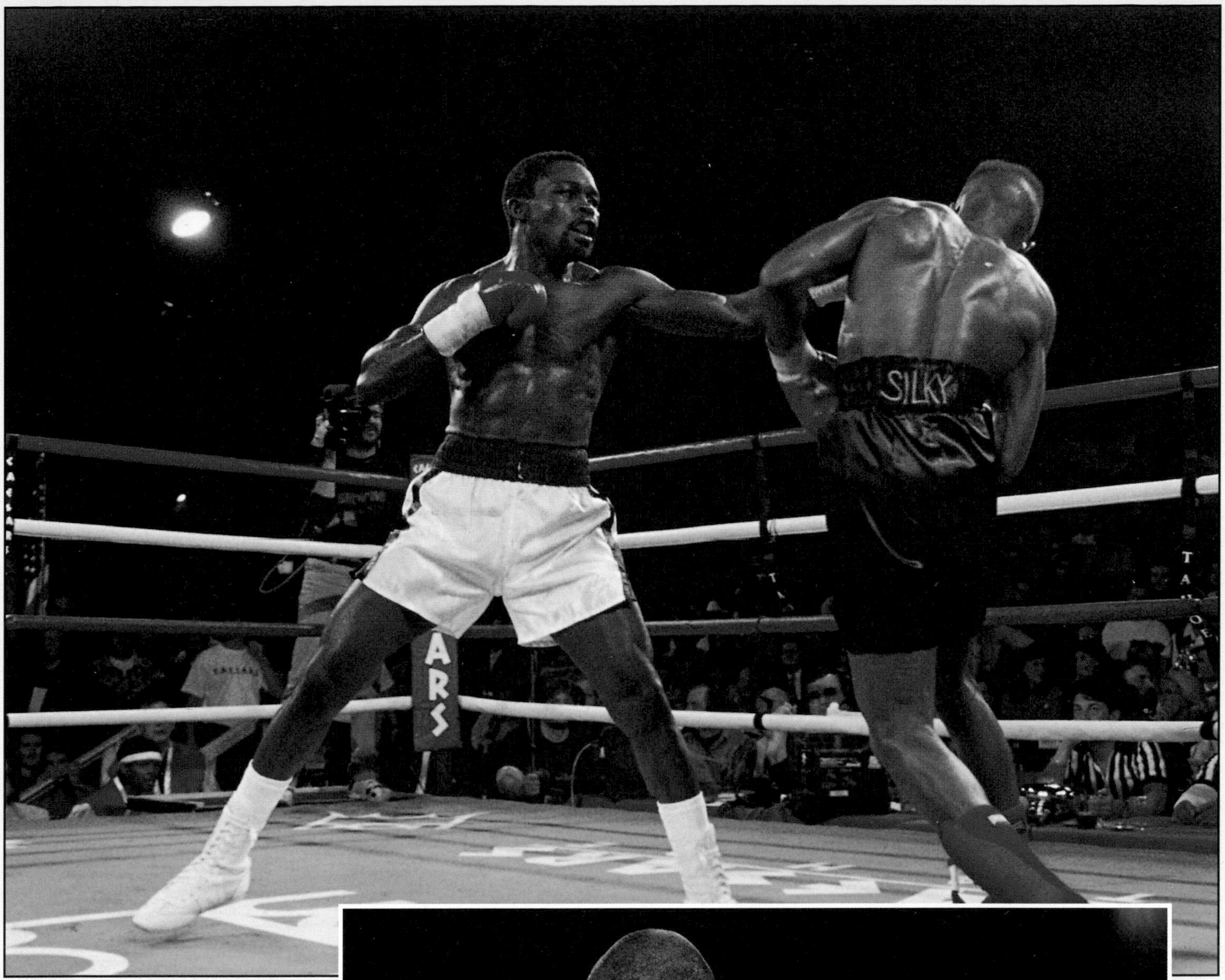

Above: Beautifully balanced, the master boxer spears Calvin Grove with a left jab in 1992.

Right: Nelson had problems with Leija in their first two meetings, drawing the first and losing the second, but he made no mistake in their third clash in Las Vegas in 1996.

MODERN GREATS

EUSEBIO PEDROZA

EUSEBIO PEDROZA was, in the truest sense of the word, a world champion. Not for him the safe defences at home with sympathetic officials and passionate crowd backing – he took his WBA featherweight title on the road, and held it through twenty defences against the best contenders available. He fought in places where world championship boxing had not been seen before, such as Papua New Guinea and St Vincent, as well as Puerto Rico, America, Korea, Japan, Venezuela, Italy and finally Britain, where Barry McGuigan ended his reign on a night of wild excitement in June 1985.

The spindly Panamanian was a boxing artist, a fast and skilful performer who made full use of his natural advantages in height and reach. (He was 5 ft 9 in, which is tall for a featherweight). He began his career as a bantamweight in 1973, under the management of Santiago Del Rio, who guided him throughout his championship era. After only fifteen fights, none of them against significant opposition, he was given a crack at the WBA bantamweight title, but was knocked out in two rounds by the hard-hitting champion Alfonso Zamora of Mexico in 1976. That was his second loss, Alfonso Perez having beaten him in three rounds in 1975, and when he was knocked out again two fights later the chances of him ever becoming an all-time great were remote.

FORM LINE

Born:	**2 March 1953, Panama City**
Height:	**5 ft 9 in**
Weight:	**116–137 lb**
Pro debut:	**1 December 1973, Panama City; Julio Garcia, won, KO Round 4**
Last fight:	**21 November 1992, Detroit; Mauro Gutierrez, lost on points, 10 rounds**
Total fights:	**49**
Wins:	**42 (25 inside schedule)**
Losses:	**6 (3 inside schedule)**
Championship:	**19 wins (11 inside record schedule), 1 draw, 2 defeats**
Titles:	**WBA featherweight champion, 1978–85**

The defeats convinced Pedroza to move up to featherweight, and the switch paid instant dividends as a trio of wins over rated opponents in 1977 earned him a match with WBA champion Cecilio Lastra of Spain. Pedroza had home advantage, and made the most of it with a 13th round stoppage on 15 April 1978. It was the start of a brilliantly successful reign as Pedroza set about proving himself the best at the weight – no easy task considering that his WBC counterparts were, in order, Danny Lopez, Salvador Sanchez, Wilfredo Gomez and Azumah Nelson.

Pedroza met every leading contender, and beat them all with a mixture of technical skill and ruthless fouls, which repeatedly brought him close to disqualification. But when he finally lost the title to McGuigan, it was in a classic contest graced by flawless sportsmanship. He retired after one more fight, but later made a brief comeback as a lightweight before embarking on a political career in Panama.

Right: The boxing artistry of Eusebio Pedroza is beautifully illustrated in this shot from his 1985 clash with Barry McGuigan: he has slipped McGuigan's jab and is poised to counter.

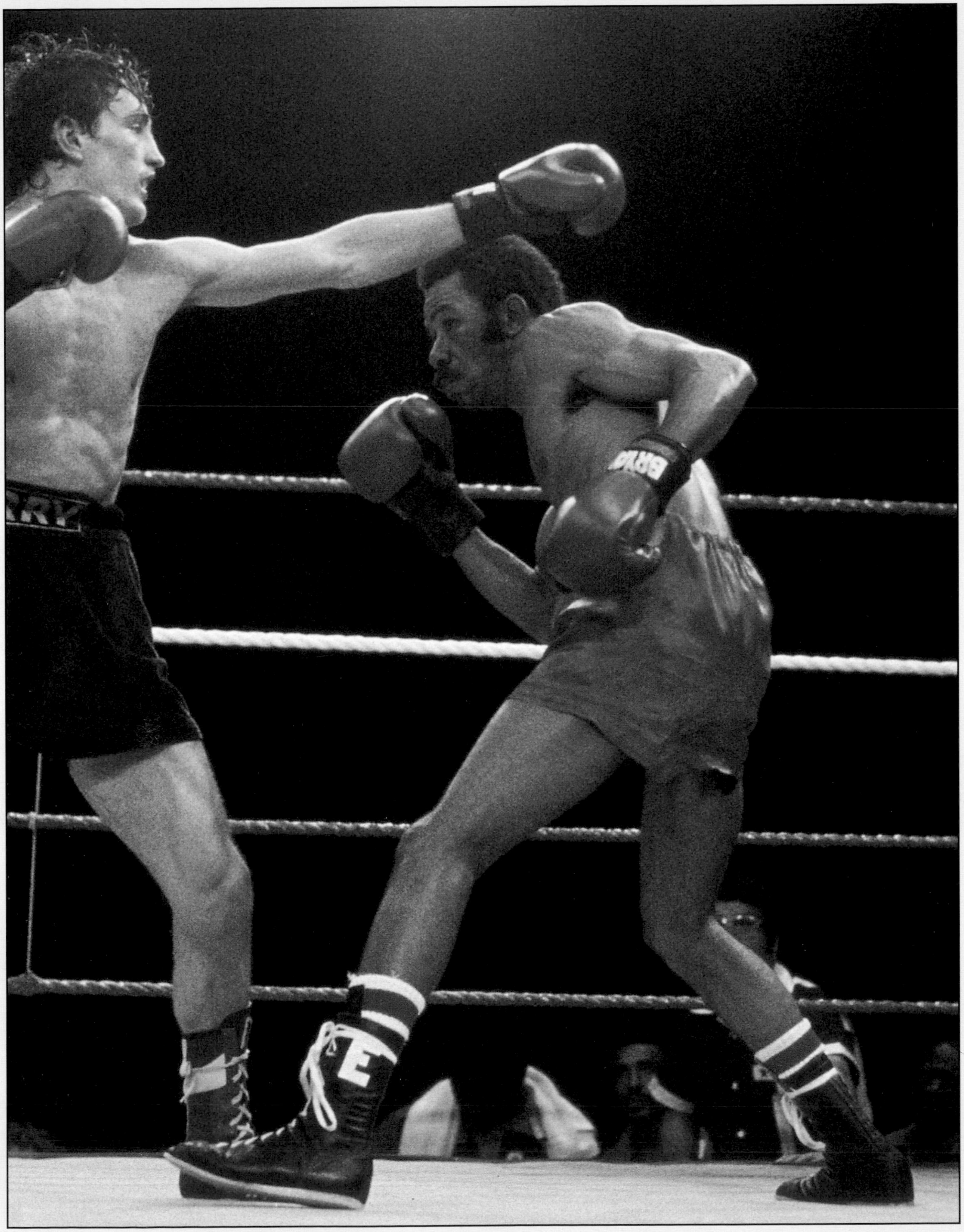

MODERN GREATS

AARON PRYOR

DRUGS destroyed Aaron Pryor, an unbeatable world champion who spent the first half of the 1980s as a million-dollar fighter and the decade's second half as a penniless wreck in the nightmare world of crack houses and jails. Few have flown so high, in all senses of the word, or fluttered to earth so abruptly, as the Cincinnati Hawk.

In his prime he was a non-stop action man whose phenomenal work-rate brought comparison with Henry Armstrong, the 1930s triple champion. When his drug abuse became common knowledge, there were cynical suggestions that his victories may have been chemically assisted, notably because of an incident in his first fight with Alexis Arguello when he was seen to imbibe from a small black bottle between rounds, the contents of which were never satisfactorily explained. But Pryor always fought that way, even back in his amateur days when he was winning the 1973 AAU lightweight title and boxing for America.

He turned pro after losing to Howard Davis in a box-off for the American Olympic team, but without big-time management it took him 26 fights to become world champion, by knocking out the veteran Colombian Antonio Cervantes in four rounds in August 1980. He was an exciting, hard-hitting performer who won only four fights on points in his 40-fight career, and all eight of his WBA title defences ended inside schedule. However, he may have impeded his own career by his insistence on staying close to home: most of his fights took place in the Cincinnati area, rather than in boxing's mainstream venues like Las Vegas or Atlantic City.

Pryor relinquished the WBA belt in December 1983 to accept the IBF's championship, but he was already hooked on drugs and, significantly, both his IBF defences went the full distance. By the time he was 29 he was burnt out and financially ruined, with a string of failed marriages behind him. He drifted away from boxing, and inevitably finished up in prison for a drugs offence. On his release he attempted a comeback, even though he was blind in one eye, but lost his perfect record to an ordinary welterweight, Bobby Joe Young. It was his only defeat, and he retired for good after one more victory.

He went into rehabilitation and, as he recounted in a moving autobiography *Flight Of The Hawk* (published in 1996), eventually found religion and won his long battle against addiction.

Above: Pryor shows off his new IBF title belt after beating Nicky Furlano in Montreal in 1984. It was the first time in 10 title fights that he had been taken the full distance.

FORM LINE

Born:	**20 October 1955, Cincinnati, Ohio**
Height:	**5ft 6 1/2 in**
Weight:	**137–148 lb**
Pro debut:	**12 November 1976, Cincinnati; Larry Smith, won, ref stopped fight Round 2**
Last fight:	**4 December 1990, Oklahoma; Roger Choate, won, ref stopped fight Round 7**
Total fights:	**40**
Wins:	**39 (35 inside schedule)**
Losses:	**1**
Championship:	**record 11 wins (9 inside schedule), no defeats**
Titles:	**WBA light-welterweight champion, 1980–4; IBF light-welterweight champion, 1984–5**

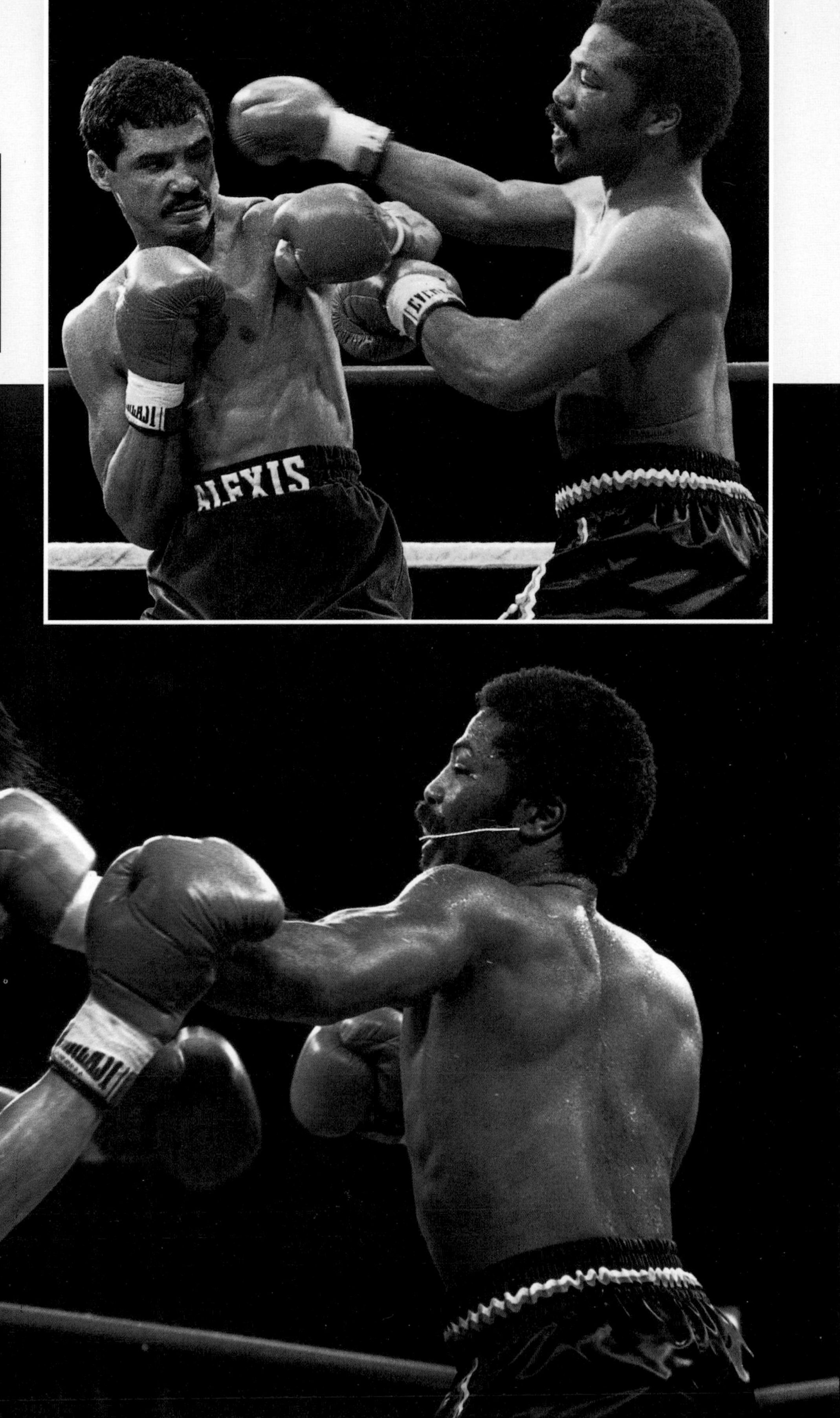

His career peak – Pryor battles to a thrilling victory over Alexis Arguello in Miami in November 1982. He was never so good again.

SKY
SPORTS
THE
Sun
PRINCE

Chapter 2

The Entertainers

SOME of the men featured here are destined for greatness: Oscar De La Hoya, Roy Jones, Pernell Whitaker and Mike McCallum have already staked their claims, while others such as Britain's precocious Naseem Hamed, Mexican puncher Ricardo Lopez or Ghana's impressive welterweight Ike Quartey have the potential to do so. But what links them is their ability to thrill a crowd – they are champions, but they are also entertainers.

ROUND

The Prince is King – Steve Robinson goes down to defeat as Naseem Hamed becomes WBO featherweight champion.

RIDDICK BOWE

Born Brownsville, New York, 10 August 1967

KNOWN as 'Big Daddy', Riddick Bowe may well be remembered as the man who ate himself out of the world heavyweight title. His gargantuan appetite was such that he even had a kitchen installed in the bedroom of his new house, built with the proceeds of his magnificent title win over Evander Holyfield in 1992. That probably contributed to his loss to Holyfield a year later, on a night made even more memorable by the unscheduled arrival in the ring of a paraglider.

Bowe, from the same Brownsville ghetto as Mike Tyson, was generally seen as Tyson's natural successor, but damaged his reputation by his refusal to face Lennox Lewis, who had stopped him in the super-heavyweight final of the 1988 Olympic Games. He came back from the Holyfield defeat to take the WBO title from Herbie Hide, but relinquished it to meet Holyfield in a decider, which he won after surviving the first knockdown of his career.

With a Tyson fight his for the asking, Bowe turned up in disgraceful condition for a routine ten-rounder against Andrew Golota at Madison Square Garden in June 1996. He was only a punch or two from defeat when Golota stupidly fouled him and was disqualified, a decision that set off the worst riot in New York boxing history.

Bowe lands a perfect left jab on perennial rival Evander Holyfield, whom he beat in two of their three meetings.

JORGE CASTRO

Born Santa Cruz, Argentina, 18 August 1967

BIG-HEARTED Argentinean Jorge Castro just never knows when he is beaten, which makes him one of the game's most entertaining performers. The flat-nosed veteran reached his century of wins late in 1996. Only five men have beaten him in an action-packed nine-year career.

He did not win any major amateur honours, although he scored a win over the Cuban world champion Carlo Garcia. His early career was spent as a light-middleweight, in which division he became Argentine and South American champion and, in 1991, went the distance with Terry Norris in a WBC title bid. Castro stepped up to middleweight and, after losing on points to Roy Jones, he went unbeaten in his next 24 fights, taking the WBA title from Reggie Johnson in August 1994.

His four successful defences include a famous come-from-behind stoppage of John David Jackson in Monterey in December 1994 when Castro, horribly cut and trailing hopelessly on points, saved the title with one spectacular punch. He lost it surprisingly a year later to Shinji Takehara, Japan's only world middleweight champion, but remains highly ranked.

In February 1997 the veteran ex-champ stepped up a division to super-middleweight to face another of the game's legends, Roberto Duran, and took a hard-earned points decision which Duran hotly disputed. He had a case: one judge did not have Castro losing a round with a score of 100-94, while another had him winning by just one point, 99-98. But at least the result kept Castro's world title hopes alive, and put him in line for another crack at a world title

He's no pin-up, but the curly-haired Castro is a real fighter.

STEVE COLLINS

Born Dublin, Eire, 21 July 1964

THE rugged Dubliner learned his trade the hard way, fighting some of the toughest middleweights in America after launching his pro career in Brockton as a stablemate of world champion Marvin Hagler. Collins reached three Irish amateur finals before winning the middleweight title in 1986 and emigrating to Boston, where he won the Irish and the USBA titles before, after only sixteen fights, he faced mighty Mike McCallum for the WBA title.

McCallum won on points in a tough fight, but Collins's reputation was made. He had another world title shot in 1992, losing a close call to Reggie Johnson for the vacant WBA title, and suffered his only other loss later that year when former world champion Sumbu Kalambay narrowly outpointed him for the European title in Italy. Since then, Collins has not looked back. He returned to Ireland, stopped Chris Pyatt in 1994 for the WBO title, and then became Ireland's first double world champion by snapping Chris Eubank's long unbeaten record to take the WBO super-middleweight title. He has since retained that against Eubank, Nigel Benn (twice), Cornelius Carr, Neville Brown and Frederic Sillier to earn international respect as one of the toughest competitors on the current scene.

Collins grinds down Benn in their first fight in 1996.

OSCAR DE LA HOYA

Born Los Angeles, 4 February 1973

DE LA HOYA is the perfect package, a handsome and articulate charmer who rates with the best pound-for-pound fighters in the business. Advertising executives and TV money-men love him because he is a 'crossover' star. He inspires equal affection from the Latin community from which he came in Los Angeles and white, middle-class America, who took him to their collective heart when he dazzled the world's best amateur lightweights to win his country's only boxing gold medal at the 1992 Olympic Games and dedicated his success to his mother, who had recently died of cancer.

De La Hoya struck an astonishing deal when he turned professional which made him a millionaire before he won his first title, and then showed a ruthless steak by dumping the managers who had brought him this far in his career. He won WBO titles at super-feather and lightweight, and added the IBF lightweight title with a brilliant second-round defeat of Mexican rival Rafael Ruelas. But his supreme triumph was over Mexico's greatest champion, Julio Cesar Chavez, whom he outclassed in four rounds in June 1996 to become WBC light-welterweight champion. It was a rare clash of the generations: the superstar of the 1980s against the man poised to dominate the 1990s.

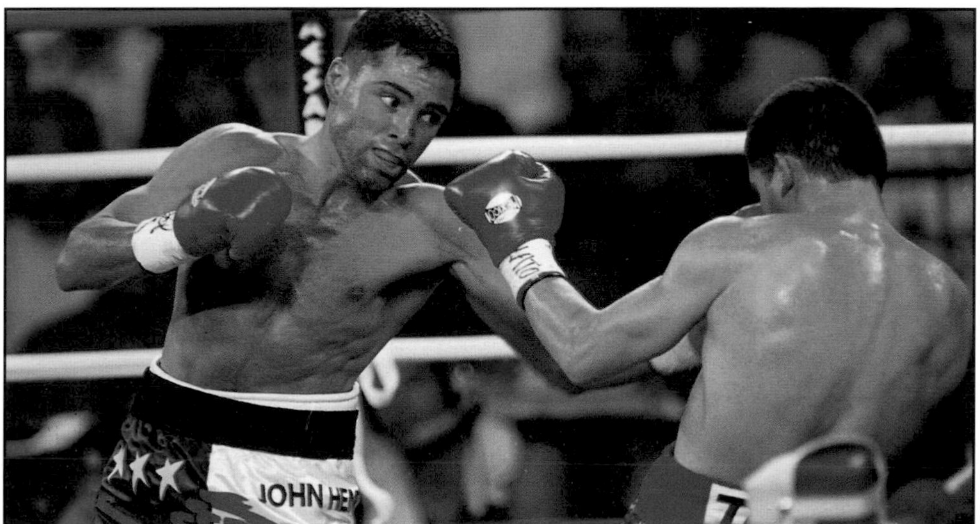

End of an era – Julio Cesar Chavez is pummelled to defeat by De La Hoya.

THE ENTERTAINERS

CHRIS EUBANK

Born Dulwich, London, 8 August 1966

British boxing had not seen the likes of the flamboyant Eubank.

PART-SHOWMAN, part-clown, part-fighter, Chris Eubank defied classification. British boxing had never seen anyone quite like the strutting, posing, flamboyant Eubank, who started his pro career in America after a troubled upbringing on the streets of South London and in assorted reform schools and secure units. He claimed to loathe boxing, yet used that expressed distaste for his profession as a marketing point for the elaborate persona he created for himself. He set out deliberately to become The Man You Love To Hate, and succeeded brilliantly.

His considerable ability in the ring, allied to Barry Hearn's promotional flair, created the Eubank phenomenon, which dominated British boxing in the first half of the 1990s. His elaborate ring entrances, which included being delivered to the ring on a crane and on a Harley Davidson, caused almost as much excitement and controversy as the fights themselves, while careful match-making ensured that his unbeaten record was preserved.

But he could really fight when he had to, as he proved in epic victories over Nigel Benn and Michael Watson to win WBO titles at, respectively, middleweight and super-middleweight. He won seventeen and drew two of his 21 WBO title fights, a British record, and retired after losing for the second time to Steve Collins – only to launch a comeback in late 1996.

PRINCE NASEEM HAMED

Born Sheffield, England, 12 February 1974

THERE is no middle ground where the self-styled 'Prince' is concerned: you either love him or loathe him, and he doesn't much care one way or the other so long as you have paid for your ticket. WBO featherweight champion at 21, the precocious Hamed is the supreme showman, an extrovert whose self-confidence often crosses the border into arrogance.

He has tricks that not even his wily old trainer Brendan Ingle could teach him: he will stare intently at an opponent's feet and then hit him flush in the face, with radar-guided accuracy, or throw punches from impossible angles while seeming to defy gravity itself. Not even he can explain how he does it, although he will cheerfully spend hours trying to. He is simply a natural, instinctive genius, utterly convinced of his own destiny to be a ring legend.

He won schools and junior ABA titles, but never competed in the senior championships because he felt, rightly, that amateur officials did not appreciate his often eccentric and always unorthodox approach to his sport. As a professional, guided by Ingle, he was an instant sensation, winning the European bantamweight title and the WBC International super-bantamweight championship before stopping Steve Robinson for the WBO belt in September 1995.

A string of spectacular defences, including a stoppage of former champion Manuel Medina, set up a unification match with IBF title-holder Tom Johnson in February 1997. It was Hamed's biggest test, in a fight shown live in America, and he finally convinced the sceptics by crushing the American in style to become a double champion. He plans to complete the four-timer by adding the WBA and WBC belts in 1997, before tackling the super-featherweights and even lightweights.

Number One – and nobody's arguing now.

BERNARD HOPKINS

Born Philadelphia, 15 January 1965

PROFESSIONAL boxing has never been known as a bastion of good taste, but Bernard Hopkins stretches the boundaries of acceptability by billing himself as 'The Executioner' and making his ring entrance in a headsman's hood, preceded by attendants carrying an axe. Luckily for Hopkins, he can usually live up to the build-up by delivering a win, as only two men have beaten him so far.

One of the losses came on his pro debut and the other was to the seemingly unbeatable Roy Jones, who outpointed him in a bid for the vacant IBF middleweight title in May 1993. Jones gave up the title to box at super-middleweight, and Hopkins came off the floor twice to earn a draw with Segundo Mercado in a tough battle for the vacant title. They were rematched, and this time Hopkins finally became champion with a seventh-round stoppage.

The Philadelphian comes from the classic background of American boxers, being reared in the ghetto and drifting into a life of crime before coming out of prison in 1988 to turn professional. He is not a showy performer, but likes to wear his opponents down methodically and is particularly effective to the body.

Hopkins batters the previously unbeaten Joe Lipsey to a fourth-round defeat in March 1996.

JULIAN JACKSON

Born St Thomas, Virgin Islands, 12 September 1960

THE ageing Jackson, who was born in September 1960, is unlikely to win a world title again but his place in boxing history is secure. By common consent, he is the hardest single-punch hitter of his generation, and is arguably even the heaviest puncher in the annals of the middleweight division.

A deeply religious family man away from the ring, he is an explosive and flamboyant performer during business hours. Time and again, he would salvage a lost cause with one dramatic punch, a quality he best demonstrated in a memorable knockout of Herol Graham to win the vacant WBC middleweight title in 1990.

He had earlier been WBA light-middleweight champion, lifting the title at the second attempt after losing a thrilling battle with Mike McCallum, who was rocked in the first round before stopping Jackson in the second.

The Virgin Islander held the middleweight crown for four defences, two of which he won inside a round, before losing it in an epic thriller against the ill-fated Gerald McClellan. In a rematch the American knocked him out in the first round, but the irrepressible Jackson bounced back to win the title again when McClellan moved up to super-middle. He finally lost it to Quincy Taylor in August 1995, on the same show as Mike Tyson's comeback.

But anyone who has knocked out 48 of his 52 victims, which was Jackson's hugely impressive total as he started his 1997 campaign, can never be entirely written off. With so many versions of the world title currently on offer, and in a division without a truly outstanding champion, Jackson will always have the traditional 'puncher's chance' of snatching yet another title.

Jackson – one of the great, instinctive punchers of modern times.

ROY JONES

Born Pensacola, Florida, 16 January 1969

ROY JONES shot to international prominence when he was the victim of the worst decision in the history of Olympic boxing, being robbed of the gold medal in the 1988 light-middleweight final against a Korean. Yet his father, who was also his manager, failed to cash in fully on the swell of public sympathy and Jones's professional career stagnated for three years before the fighter went his own way.

Since then, the rewards have been dramatic: world titles at middle, super-middle and light-heavy, and universal acclaim as the best pound-for-pound boxer currently active. Jones can do it all: box, brawl, punch in clusters so fast that a slow-motion reply is necessary to count the blows, and hit with concussive one-punch power.

He won his first two titles by outclassing Bernard Hopkins and James Toney, two of the most intimidating men in the business, and closed 1996 by winning every round from 'The Bodysnatcher', Mike McCallum, for the vacant WBC light-heavyweight title. He plans to move through the divisions to win the cruiserweight and even the heavyweight titles, and has performed with such effortless assurance so far that it would be foolish to bet against him doing just that.

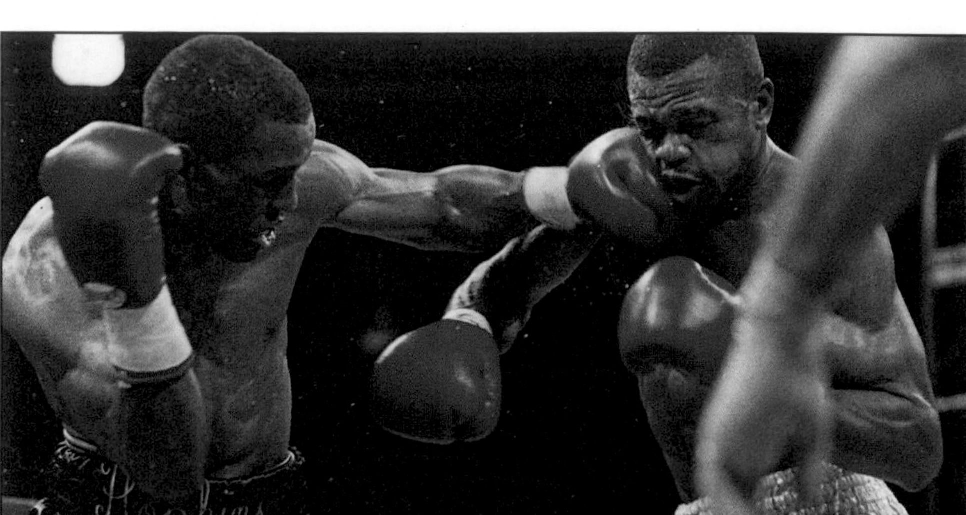

Jones (right) decisively outscored Bernard Hopkins to win his first world title.

LENNOX LEWIS

Born London, 2 September 1965

LENNOX LEWIS became WBC heavyweight champion by default, when Riddick Bowe – the man Lewis had stopped in two rounds to win the Olympic super-heavyweight title in 1988 – relinquished the belt rather than defend against him. The WBC proclaimed the English-born, Canadian-raised Lewis champion on the basis of his crushing second-round defeat of Razor Ruddock in a final eliminator in October 1992, and he retained his championship three times before Oliver McCall shocked him in 1994. It remains his only setback in 31 contests. The Londoner is sometimes lazy in action, but has the punch that matters: he has won 26 contests inside schedule.

Lewis boxed as an amateur for Canada, but took the game's insiders by surprise when he joined Frank Maloney, a small-time London manager, rather than one of the major camps. Maloney steered him to the European, British and Commonwealth titles, and Lewis responded with exemplary loyalty by resisting the most determined efforts of Don King to lure him away.

He finally regained the WBC title in February 1997, stopping McCall in the fifth round of a bizarre encounter.

Razor trimmed – Lewis sends Ruddock crashing to defeat.

RICARDO LOPEZ

Born Mexico City, Mexico, 25 July 1966

HIS nickname tells the whole story: Ricardo 'Finito' Lopez is indeed among the game's great 'finishers', a wicked-punching craftsman who never lets an opponent off the hook and who had, to the end of 1996, stopped or knocked out 34 of the 44 men he had faced in an unbeaten career.

Were he a few stones heavier, Lopez would be one of boxing's mega-stars, up there with Roy Jones, Mike Tyson and Oscar De La Hoya. But he is a strawweight, the sport's lightest category, and so his extraordinary record and achievements rate little attention outside his native Mexico.

He won the WBC title in October 1990, and only three of his seventeen title challengers have lasted the distance, even though he has consistently faced the best available contenders. Like all big punchers, he has been plagued by recurring hand trouble, but has remained a busy and hard-working champion as he enters the twelfth year of a remarkable career. Lopez is comfortably on course to emulate Rocky Marciano's record of 49 straight wins, though unlike Marciano, Lopez is a stylish boxer as well as a chilling hitter. He was voted WBC Fighter of the Year for 1996.

Another one bites the dust – Lopez looks invincible as another contender is rescued.

MIKE McCALLUM

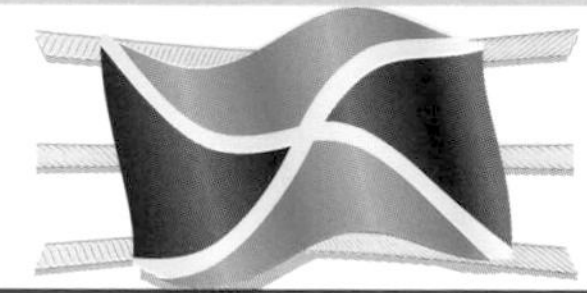

Born Kingston, Jamaica, 7 December 1956

MIKE McCALLUM was still good enough, at 40, to go the full twelve rounds with superstar Roy Jones for the vacant WBC light-heavyweight title in his last fight of 1996. That is an accurate measure of his ability, and even though the veteran was clearly outpointed he still earned Jones's respect. If it was indeed the Last Hurrah for the ageing Jamaican, at least he went out with style.

McCallum, whose fierce body punching earned him the nickname 'The Bodysnatcher', has been a major figure on the world fight scene since 1984, when he won the vacant WBA light-middleweight title. His six defences included stunning defeats of Julian Jackson, Don Curry and Milton McCrory, all outstanding world champions, and then he moved up to middleweight to become WBA champion at the second attempt in 1989.

Politics cost him the title, when the WBA stripped him for meeting IBF champion James Toney (they fought a disputed draw). McCallum promptly stepped up two more weights, bypassing the super-middleweights to beat Jeff Harding for the WBC light-heavyweight title, which Fabrice Tiozzo took off him in his second defence.

The veteran was given one last chance at the big-time in February 1997 when he faced his old rival James Toney for the third time. Most experts thought McCallum had deserved to win at least one of their previous meetings, but he had to settle for a draw and a disputed points loss. But there was no argument about the outcome this time, as Toney, himself a shadow of the force he had been when they last met, won a comfortable decision which clearly points the way towards retirement for the classy Jamaican.

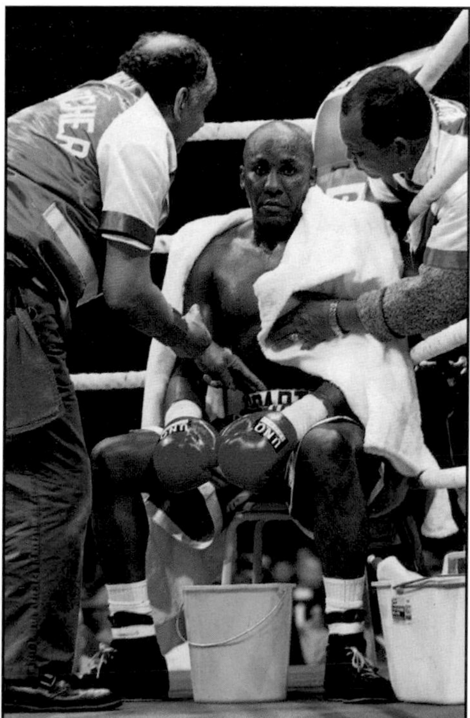

McCallum and his corner team exude old-pro calmness and composure.

THE ENTERTAINERS

WAYNE McCULLOUGH

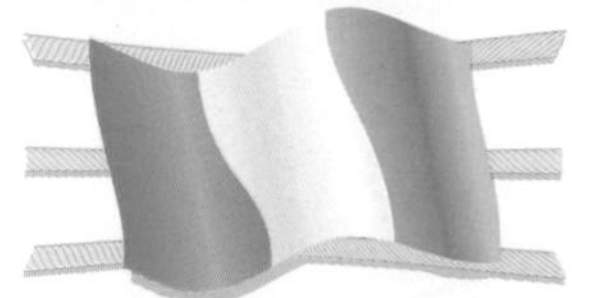

Born Belfast, Ireland, 7 July 1970

Danish challenger Johnny Bredahl (right) was swept aside in eight rounds of McCullough's first bantamweight title defence.

THE single-minded dedication that persuaded Wayne McCullough to leave Belfast, settle in Las Vegas and gamble his future on a link-up with a young and inexperienced manager, Mat Tinley, paid off handsomely when the Irishman earned a record purse for a bantamweight challenger in his June 1995 victory over the rugged Japanese WBC title-holder Yasuei Yakashiji. Tinley, an executive with Prime TV, secured McCullough TV coverage for all his twenty unbeaten fights and engaged boxing's greatest trainer, Eddie Futch, to supervise his development from Olympic silver medallist to professional world champion. Futch and his assistant Thel Torrance have added guile to McCullough's exuberant style, but McCullough's love of a punch-up is the key to his popularity.

Thrilling victories over former world champions Victor Rabanales and Fabrice Benichou earned him his crack at Yakashiji's title in Tokyo. He retained the bantamweight title twice, the second a gruelling points win over Jose Luis Bueno in which he took so much punishment that he decided to move up a division to challenge Daniel Zaragoza for the WBC super-bantamweight title, which saw him lose for the first time when Zaragoza outpointed him in January 1997.

TERRY NORRIS

Born Lubbock, Texas, 17 June 1967

IT SOUNDS a contradiction to describe a boxer as both consistent and unpredictable, yet the adjectives can legitimately be applied to WBC and IBF light-middleweight champion Terry Norris. The stylish Texan has been a world champion on and off since 1990, but has also figured in some shocking upsets and bizarre endings. He won the WBC title by flattening John Mugabi in the first round, having previously lost in two rounds to Julian Jackson in a thriller for the WBA championship.

Norris made nine defences before Simon Brown, a former welterweight champion, knocked him out in a major surprise. He regained the title from Brown six months later, then lost it again to Luis Santana, who was declared the winner while lying on a stretcher, ostensibly having been incapacitated by a rabbit punch.

Astonishingly, the same thing happened in the rematch, but Norris finally got it right at the third attempt by stopping Santana in two rounds in August 1985. In December that year, he added the IBF title by beating Paul Vaden. Norris's other championship victims include Sugar Ray Leonard, whom he trounced at Madison Square Garden in 1991 to send Leonard into retirement yet again.

Norris, whose brother Orlin was WBA cruiserweight champion in 1993–5, has already stablished himself as the outstanding performer in the 35-year history of the light-middleweight division, but he has still to face his toughest test. That will come when he defends against the explosive-punching IBF welterweight champion Felix Trinidad, in one of the most eagerly awaited championship pairings of 1997.

Norris, backed by Don King, celebrates the win over Paul Varden which made him a double champion.

IKE QUARTEY

Born Accra, Ghana, 27 November 1969

THE heavy-fisted, unbeaten Ghanaian has been slow to earn acceptance in America because most of his major fights have been in France, but he is such an exciting performer that he looks sure to make the breakthrough in 1997. The WBA welterweight champion lacks the concussive, one-punch power of IBF rival Felix Trinidad, but his remorseless attacks tend to wear opponents down so successfully that only four men have taken him the distance in 33 fights to the end of 1996.

Quartey was an outstanding amateur, competing in the 1988 Olympic Games. Curiously, one of his many brothers, also called Ike, won the Empire Games light-welterweight gold medal in 1962, beating the legendary Scot Dick McTaggart en route.

Young Ike boxed in the world junior championships without success, but adapted quickly to the pro game and won the Ghanaian and All-African titles before lifting the vacant WBC International title in March 1992. Two years later, after moving permanently to France under the management of the Acaries brothers, he stopped the previously unbeaten Venezuelan Crisanto Espana for the WBA title in June 1994.

Popular winner – Quartey is chaired by his fellow-Ghanaians after winning the WBA title.

FRANKIE RANDALL

Born Birmingham, Alabama, 25 September 1961

THE icy precision of Frankie Randall's boxing has earned him the nickname 'The Surgeon', and those he has dissected in an up-and-down career include the greatest fighter of his generation, Julio Cesar Chavez. Randall will always be remembered as the man who snapped the Mexican's fabulous unbeaten run, flooring him in the process to take the WBC light-welterweight title.

It was a stunning performance by a 15-1 underdog, and he proved it was no fluke by giving Chavez nightmares in the rematch before losing on a controversial technical decision. Beating Chavez was the unquestioned high point of a career punctuated by drug addiction, alcoholism and a jail term. Randall always had championship potential, but seemed destined never to fulfil it.

He was a top-ranked lightweight contender when he was jailed for drug dealing in 1990, but worked his way back up the ratings at light-welterweight to earn his date with Chavez. After losing the rematch he won and lost the WBA version of the title. By the end of 1996 his future was uncertain, with reports that his career was again threatened by alcoholism. Whatever happens, that win over Chavez has earned him his own piece of immortality.

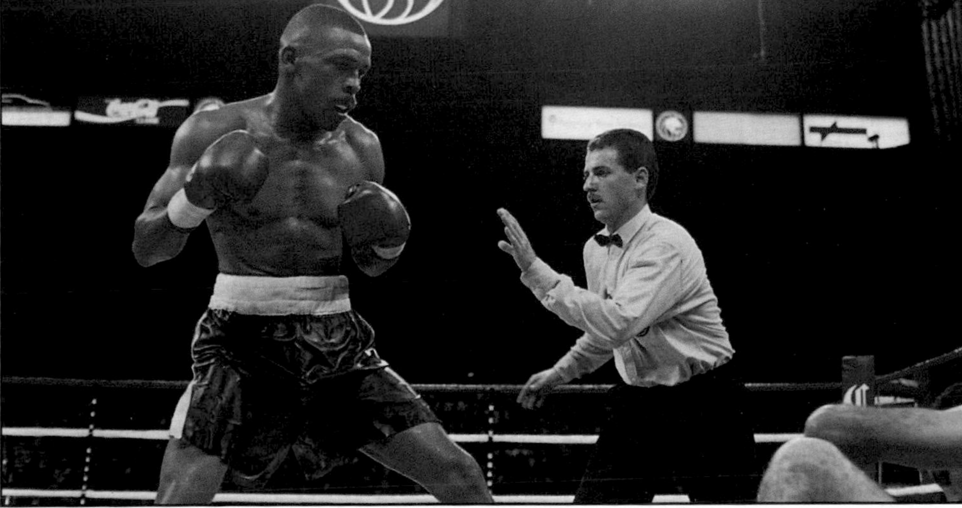

Randall knocks Juan Martin Coggi out of the championship picture in 1994.

JOHNNY TAPIA

Born Albuquerque, New Mexico, 13 February 1967

ALBUQUERQUE'S best-known world champion, light-heavyweight legend Bob Foster, has been a deputy sheriff for nearly 30 years. His fellow-townsman, Johnny Tapia, is from the other side of the tracks, one of boxing's Bad Boys who has spent as much time out of action through drug problems as he has in actively pursuing his career. He has also been arrested for an assortment of offences including assaulting his wife and carrying a weapon, but seems finally to be straightening himself out and has been 'clean' for over two years.

He was a two-time Golden Gloves champion at light-flyweight and flyweight in 1983 and 1984, but his drug habit took hold and kept him out of the sport for three years. He turned pro in 1988, and his widely publicized problems helped make him a big attraction. He drew his pro debut but then ran up 21 straight wins, stopping Roland Gomez for the USBA super-flyweight title in 1990 and retaining it four times before his drug habit resurfaced.

Tapia made rapid progress on his return from a near-four-year layoff in March 1994, and six wins that year culminated in a WBO title win over Henry Martinez. He has been a busy, colourful and entertaining champion, retaining his title eight times to the end of 1996.

Tapia's priority now is a showdown with Albuquerque rival Danny Romero, who holds the IBF flyweight title and is the antithesis of Tapia in lifestyle as well as ring technique. It is the biggest all-American match in that weight bracket for many years, but Bob Arum, who promotes them both, insists he will not stage the match in their hometown because of the dangers of clashes between rival fans.

Bad boy, good fighter – that's Johnny Tapia.

FELIX TRINIDAD

Born Cupoy Alto, Puerto Rico, 10 January 1973

EVERYBODY loves a puncher, which explains the popularity of the tall, rangy Felix Trinidad. The Puerto Rican is an explosive hitter, and in ten defences of the IBF welterweight title he won in June 1993, only the cagey veteran Hector Camacho has managed to take him the full distance. But Trinidad can also be hit, and has sometimes needed to come off the floor to win – notably in a non-stop thriller against Yori Boy Campos in Las Vegas in 1994. The son of a fighter by the same name who once faced the great featherweight champion Salvador Sanchez, Trinidad was just seventeen when he started his professional career in 1990. He stopped eleven of his first fourteen opponents to earn a world ranking, and survived a first-round knockdown against Alberto Cortes to win their eliminator contest in Paris in October 1992.

His world title chance came against Maurice Blocker, a fine craftsman from Washington who was a class above anyone Trinidad had previously met, but the challenger – barely twenty – destroyed him in two rounds. Since then he has retained the title against top-grade contenders like Oba Carr, Roger Turner, Camacho, Larry Barnes and Freddie Pendleton, the former lightweight champion.

Action from Trinidad's thrilling victory over Yori Campos (left) in 1994.

KOSTA TSZYU

Born Serov, Russia, 19 September 1969

THE pig-tailed Tszyu, from Serov, was the first Russian to become a major international star after the legalization of pro boxing in his home country – but he did it under the Australian flag. Tszyu had defected while on tour with the Russian national team, and turned professional in Sydney under local promoter Bill Mordey. The hard-punching southpaw had compiled a remarkable amateur record of 269 wins in 272 fights, winning five national titles, two European gold medals and the world championship in 1991. Mordey moved him along quickly as a pro, and in only his fourth fight Tszyu clearly outpointed the former WBC featherweight champion Juan LaPorte. Two more world champions, Sammy Fuentes and Livingston Bramble, were beaten in his sixth and tenth fights respectively as the Russian raced up the world rankings.

His chance came against IBF title-holder Jake Rodriguez in Las Vegas in January 1995, and the Puerto Rican was floored five times as Tszyu battered him to defeat in the sixth round. But a promotional dispute that saw him break with Mordey prevented him from capitalizing on that success, although his career is picking up speed again and he had retained the title four times by the end of 1996.

IBF champion Jake Rodriguez crumbles under Tszyu's assault in Las Vegas in 1995.

PERNELL WHITAKER

Born Norfolk, Virginia, 2 January 1964

Whitaker (left) was robbed by this draw with Julio Chavez.

SLICK-BOXING Pernell Whitaker would have been a world champion in any era, but the profusion of championships available in today's game has enabled him to collect titles at every weight from lightweight to light-middleweight, a span of 19 lb. Despite his remarkable record, the US public has not warmed to Whitaker's southpaw skills: they tend to prefer blood-and-thunder performers.

To European eyes, however, he is a delight. He turned pro after winning the lightweight gold medal at the 1984 Olympic Games, and has lost only twice since then. The first was by points to Jose Luis Ramirez in Whitaker's first attempt at the WBC lightweight title, generally considered an outrageous robbery, and the second was by Oscar De La Hoya for the WBC welterweight title in April 1997.

Whitaker won the IBF, WBC and WBA lightweight titles before moving up to win the IBF light-welterweight and WBC welterweight titles. The only other blemish on his record came in a welterweight defence against Julio Cesar Chavez, who was 'gifted' a draw. Whitaker, known as 'Sweet Pea', won his fourth championship in 1995 by outpointing WBA light-middleweight champion Julio Cesar Vasquez, but immediately relinquished it.

Chapter 3

ROUND

The Legends

BOXING fans will always argue about the order in which the heavyweight giants are ranked, but never about the names on the list: Ali, Louis, Dempsey, Marciano and the others are automatic choices for anyone's all-time top ten. We have side-stepped controversy by recalling, in strict alphabetical order, the men and their deeds, and we leave you to debate their relative merits.

'I shocked the world, I shocked the world!' Cassius Clay can hardly believe it himself as the once-fearsome Sonny Liston quits on his stool at the end of the sixth round, leaving the wide-eyed Clay heavyweight champion at 22.

MUHAMMAD ALI

MUHAMMAD ALI has always been defiantly his own person, and yet, paradoxically, he has also been all things to all men. To those who cherish grace, courage, originality and athleticism, he once represented the acceptable face of boxing and a triumphant justification for its existence; but to those who are uneasy about the sport's long-term consequences for its participants he now embodies a powerful case for its abolition.

In his prime, he was an icon for black Americans and an ogre for their redneck, racist neighbours; a draft-dodging coward to right-wingers, or to those on the left, a martyr who contemptuously tossed away a fortune rather than take part in a war whose justification he was brave enough to question.

Even his name was divisive. Was he Cassius Marcellus Clay, the name under which his birth was registered, or Muhammad Ali, the Muslim name he adopted after winning the heavyweight title from Sonny Liston in 1964? Your answer would depend on your position on the racial and political spectrum, but for most Europeans his decision to discard his 'slave name' brought the first realization that black Americans had been denied even their historical identity.

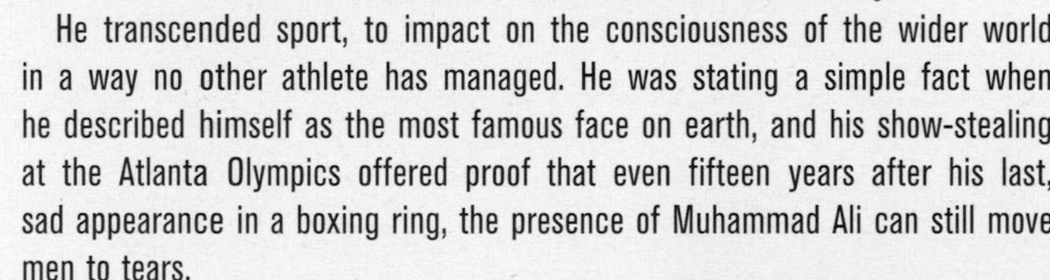

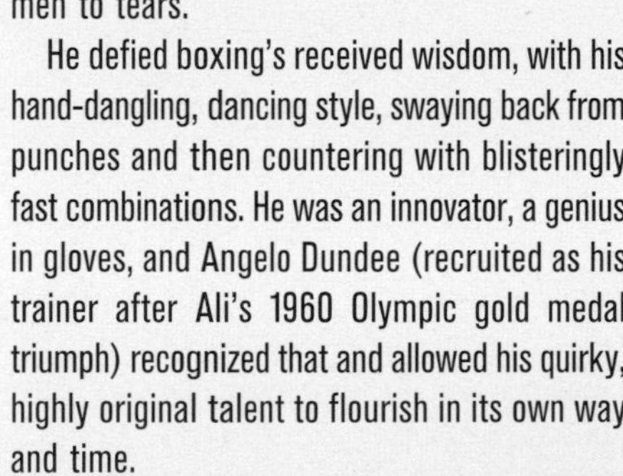

He transcended sport, to impact on the consciousness of the wider world in a way no other athlete has managed. He was stating a simple fact when he described himself as the most famous face on earth, and his show-stealing at the Atlanta Olympics offered proof that even fifteen years after his last, sad appearance in a boxing ring, the presence of Muhammad Ali can still move men to tears.

He defied boxing's received wisdom, with his hand-dangling, dancing style, swaying back from punches and then countering with blisteringly fast combinations. He was an innovator, a genius in gloves, and Angelo Dundee (recruited as his trainer after Ali's 1960 Olympic gold medal triumph) recognized that and allowed his quirky, highly original talent to flourish in its own way and time.

The world had never seen a heavyweight quite like Clay/Ali, and his flamboyant personality and colourful fight predictions – naming, in doggerel verse, the round in which his opponent would fall – made wonderful media copy. When he outclassed the fearsome Liston, forcing him to retire in his corner after six rounds, he proved there was substance to go with the style.

Still a star – Ali's appearance at the opening ceremony of the 1996 Atlanta Olympics was a show-stopper.

FORM LINE

Born:	**17 January 1942, Louisville, Kentucky.**
Height:	**6ft 3 in**
Weight:	**186–230 lb**
Pro debut:	**29 October 1960, Louisville; Tunney Hunsaker, won on pts, 6 rounds**
Last fight:	**11 December 1981, Nassau, Bahamas; Trevor Berbick, lost on pts, 10 rounds**
Total fights:	**61**
Wins:	**56 (19 inside schedule)**
Losses:	**5 (1 inside schedule)**
Champ. record:	**22 wins, 3 defeats**
Titles:	**3 times world heavyweight champion, 1964–8, 1974–8, 1978–9**

Ali loved the good things in life, but when the time came to train he worked as hard as any champion in history . . . and Bundini Brown, the man who coined the immortal 'Butterfly' slogan, was never far away.

He became an authentic world champion, taking the title out of America for defences in Canada, Britain and Germany before, in 1967, his refusal to accept induction for military service in the Vietnam War caused him to be stripped of the championship he had retained nine times. He was out of the ring for three years, during which American public opinion swung overwhelmingly to his side, and was finally relicensed in 1970.

Joe Frazier, who had claimed the title in his absence, beat him in a magnificent clash in 1971, but Ali persisted and, in 1974, regained the title in a huge upset by knocking out George Foreman in Zaire. He made another ten defences before Leon Spinks, a gap-toothed novice, outscored him in Las Vegas in 1978.

Seven months later, Ali danced his way to an unprecedented third title when he trounced Spinks in New Orleans. He retired, but the financial demands of the huge entourage who had attached themselves to him drove him back for a pathetic challenge for Larry Holmes's WBC title. Even that was not the end: Trevor Berbick, a Jamaican of limited skills, battered him for ten rounds in Nassau in December 1981.

Like too many old fighters, he is now paying the brutal price demanded of those who linger too long in this harshest of sports. Most of them suffer in obscurity, but for Ali the cheers will never fade.

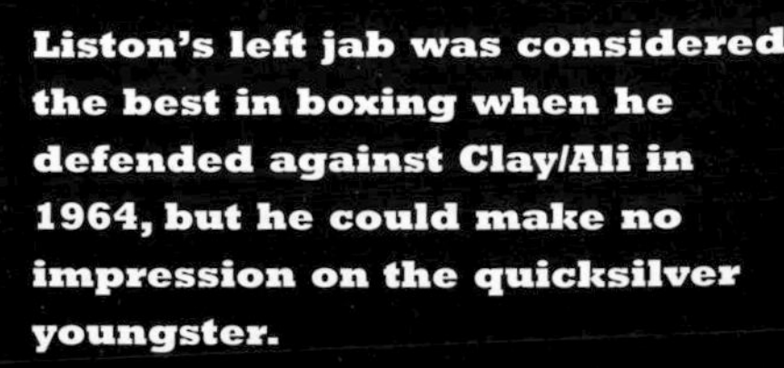
Liston's left jab was considered the best in boxing when he defended against Clay/Ali in 1964, but he could make no impression on the quicksilver youngster.

JACK DEMPSEY

THERE WAS an aura of barely controlled violence about Jack Dempsey which even now, over 70 years after he threw his last punch, communicates itself clearly through the flickering black-and-white images of the screen. He was the epitome of the fighting man, a raw-boned fury in the ring who remained, to the end of his long life, irresistibly glamorous outside it. He became the symbol of his era, the unrestrained, hedonistic Roaring Twenties. Yet his roots were in a harder time, in the pre-war mining towns of Montana, Colorado and Utah where he fought for cents and dollars in saloons and lived in hobo camps by the side of the railroad tracks.

He was born, one of nine children, in the Colorado town later immortalized by his nickname, the Manassa Mauler, and was christened William Harrison Dempsey. He borrowed his ring name from his elder brother Bernard, who had himself taken it in honour of the legendary middleweight champion nonpareil, Jack Dempsey. There was no formal training or amateur apprenticeship for young Dempsey: he picked up what he could from sparring with Bernie, and then did what so many of his impoverished compatriots were doing at that time – he rode the rails across America looking for work and taking fights where he could find them.

In 1914, when he was nineteen, he earned $3.50 for his first 'official' fight – seven short years later, he would feature in boxing's first million-dollar match. The catalyst was Jack 'Doc' Kearns, a brilliant manager and manipulator who took over Dempsey's plodding career in 1918 and transformed him into a legend. Jack had won just three of his first eight fights in 1917, yet lost only one of 21 under Kearns's guidance in 1918. Knockouts of Fred Fulton, Battling Levinsky, Carl Morris and Gunboat Smith announced his arrival as a serious contender, yet he was so much lighter (by 56 lb) than the giant champion Jess Willard that he looked like a boy against a man when they met for the title in Toledo, Ohio on 4 July 1919.

Dempsey swamped Willard, flooring him seven times in the first round with a display of unparalleled ferocity. He would stand directly over the fallen champion after each knockdown, and hammer him again as he rose. Dempsey had bet his entire purse on a first-round victory, and left the ring celebrating only to be recalled and told that the bell had interrupted the count on the final knockdown. Willard survived until the third round, taking a frightening beating.

Willard had been inactive for three years before facing Dempsey, but the new champion reactivated the title with three defences in ten months, including his million-dollar match with French war hero Georges Carpentier, whom he knocked out in four thrilling rounds. He did not fight again until 1923, when he bankrupted the town of Shelby, Montana which had bankrolled his defence against Tommy Gibbons. Dempsey

Tommy Gibbons (left) stood up to Dempsey for the full 15 rounds in their 1923 title fight in Shelby, Montana.

FORM LINE	
Born:	**24 June 1895, Manassa, Colorado**
Height:	**6ft 3/4 in**
Weight:	**170–195 lb**
Pro debut:	**17 August 1914, Ramona, Colorado; Young Herman, draw, 6 rounds**
Last fight:	**22 September 1927, Chicago; Gene Tunney, lost on pts, 10 rounds**
Total fights:	**79**
Wins:	**59 (49 inside schedule)**
Losses:	**6 (1 inside schedule), 8 draws, 6 No Decisions**
Champ. record:	**6 wins, 2 defeats**
Titles:	**World heavyweight champion, 1919–26**

won on points, but the promotion was a disaster and poor Gibbons never got paid. After beating Luis Firpo in two brutal rounds in September 1923, he was inactive for three years before facing the ex-Marine Gene Tunney in Philadelphia on 23 September 1926.

Tunney outboxed him easily, and beat him again a year later in the famous Battle Of the Long Count. Dempsey floored him in the seventh, but stood over him instead of obeying the new rule which required him to go to a neutral corner. Tunney took full advantage of the extra few seconds, and recovered quickly to win on points. Dempsey never fought again, apart from a few exhibition tours, but his popularity remained undiminished until his death on 31 May 1983.

Right: Jess Willard had no chance against the rampaging Dempsey, but he fought with extraordinary courage to last three rounds, surviving seven knockdowns in the first round. 'I've got $100,000 and a farm in Kansas', he kept repeating to his seconds as they helped him from the ring.

Below: The end for Georges Carpentier as the Frenchman, really only a light-heavyweight, is knocked out in the fourth round of boxing's first million-dollar match.

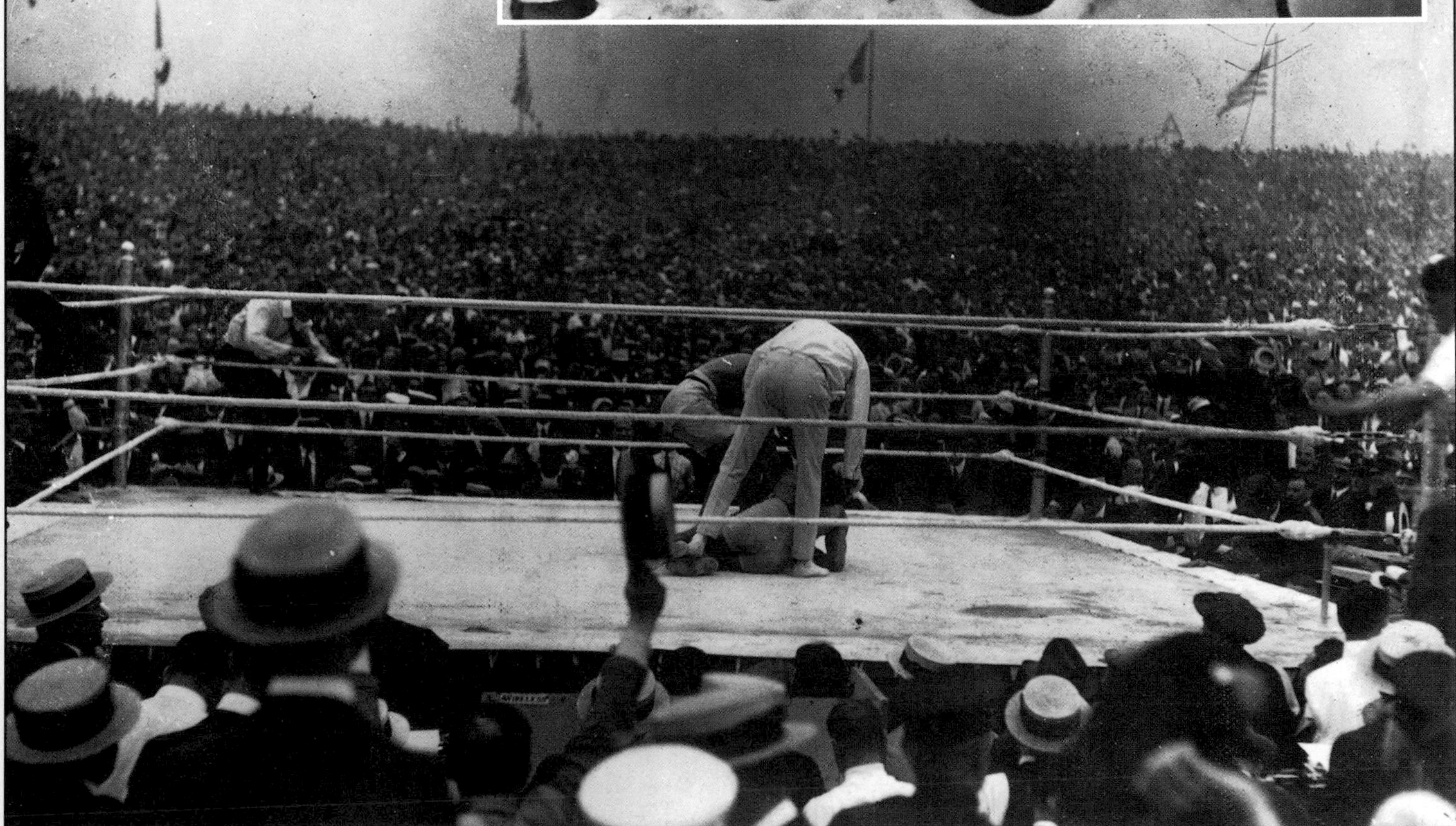

THE LEGENDS

JOE FRAZIER

NO FIGHTER in history had a more appropriate nickname than 'Smokin' Joe' Frazier. The man exuded snorting, snarling aggression, like a bull pawing the dust in the arena as he waits to attack, and he had a temper to match. It could be said that he was unlucky to be a contemporary of Muhammad Ali's, that his lustre is dimmed by Ali's shadow, but without each other neither Frazier nor Ali would have become ring legends. Great fighters need great opponents to bring out the best in them, and they served that role for each other. Their styles, like their personalities and attitudes, could not have been more different, but that only made their long and fierce rivalry all the more fascinating.

While Ali came from a comfortable middle-class background, Frazier was born into poverty in Beaufort, South Carolina. His family followed the traditional sharecropper's route north to Philadelphia in search of a better life, but money was always scarce. Joe already had a young family of his own to keep when, as a 20-year-old, he was called onto the American Olympic team as a replacement for the injured Buster Mathis and won the gold medal in Tokyo. He was working in a slaughter-house at the time, but became a full-time fighter on his return from the Games through the backing of a sponsorship group called Cloverlay Inc., who sold shares in his management and paid him a weekly salary.

Freed of financial worry, and trained first by Yank Durham and then by Eddie Futch, Frazier was beating top contenders like Oscar Bonavena, Eddie Machen, Doug Jones and George Chuvalo within two years after making his pro debut, and when the title was stripped from Muhammad Ali for his refusal to join the Army, Frazier stopped his old amateur rival Mathis to win New York recognition as champion. Jimmy Ellis, Ali's regular sparmate, won the WBA tournament involving most of the other leading challengers, but retired after four rounds when he faced Frazier for the undisputed title in February 1970.

A year later came his biggest test. Ali was relicensed, and he and Frazier clashed in an epic encounter which, for the first time, involved two undefeated champions. Frazier left-hooked him to the floor in the 15th to clinch a points win, but after two more mediocre defences he was blasted to a stunning second-round defeat by George Foreman. Ali took revenge in a twelve-rounder in 1974, but Frazier bounced back with stoppages of Jerry Quarry and Ellis again to secure a third meeting with Ali, this time for the title that Ali had regained from Foreman. That was the Thrilla In Manila, arguably the greatest heavyweight title fight of all time. Frazier fought himself to a standstill, and trainer Eddie Futch pulled him out at the end of the 14th round.

Above: Mean and moody – Joe Frazier's career was built on raw aggression.

FORM LINE

Born:	**12 January 1944, Beaufort, South Carolina**
Height:	**5ft $11^1/_2$ in**
Weight:	**200–220 lb**
Pro debut:	**16 August 1965, Philadelphia; Woody Goss, won, KO Round 1**
Last fight:	**8 December 1981, Chicago; Floyd Cummings, draw, 10 rounds**
Total fights:	**37**
Wins:	**32 (27 inside schedule)**
Losses:	**4 (3 inside schedule), 1 draw**
Champ. record:	**10 wins, 2 defeats**
Titles:	**World heavyweight champion (New York version), 1968–70; undisputed champion, 1970–3**

That effectively finished Frazier, and he was hammered in five rounds by Foreman next time out. There was just one more fight, an embarrassing ten-round draw with Floyd Cummings in an ill-judged comeback attempt five years later. He retired to become a manager and trainer.

Above: Facing his fate... Frazier gets the Evil Eye from George Foreman at the weigh-in for their 1973 title fight in Jamaica.

Right: His finest hour... Frazier on the way to victory over Ali in their 1971 showdown in Madison Square Garden.

THE LEGENDS

JACK JOHNSON

EVEN IN death, Jack Johnson continues to fascinate, tantalize and tease. He is one of the few fighters from boxing's early years whose talent can still be appreciated at this distance in time, a defensive genius whose moves anticipated Muhammad Ali by half a century. Yet he is also the only man in history to admit openly to having thrown a fight for the heavyweight championship of the world, which, if true, qualifies him for the Rogues' Gallery rather than the Hall Of Fame.

He was a fiercely controversial figure throughout his professional life, a rebel who went out of his way to infuriate White America in an era when black men who shared his preference for white women often finished up on the end of a rope. He was the first black heavyweight champion, whose coronation in 1908 prompted a wave of race riots and lynchings that was repeated after each of his major victories. Like so many other great black fighters who preceded and followed him, he was kept waiting for years for a title shot and, given the opportunity, would probably have been champion as early as 1905.

But the infamous 'colour bar', put up by John L. Sullivan and maintained by his successors, was firmly in place and the best that Johnson and his fellow blacks, like Sam Langford, Joe Jeanette, Sam McVey and the rest, could hope for was to fight each other in a protracted series that often extended to more than twenty meetings with the same opponent. He turned pro at nineteen in 1897, after a spell as a docker in his hometown of Galveston, and won the so-called 'Negro heavyweight championship' by beating Denver Ed Martin in 1903.

Eventually, he was able to persuade white contenders like Jack Monroe, Bill Lang, Fireman Jim Flynn and ex-champ Bob Fitzsimmons to face him, and as he beat them all his case for a title chance became unanswerable. Yet champion after champion avoided him, until he eventually chased the current incumbent, Tommy Burns, across the world to Britain and then to Australia, where on 26 December 1908 Johnson tormented him for fourteen rounds before the police intervened to stop the fight.

FORM LINE

Born:	**31 March 1878, Galveston, Texas**
Height:	**6 ft $1^1/_4$ in**
Weight:	**188–221 lb**
Pro debut:	**1897 (date unknown), Galveston; Jim Rocks, won, KO Round 4**
Last fight:	**15 May 1928, Kansas City; Bill Hartwell, lost, KO Round 7**
Total fights:	**105**
Wins:	**68 (40 inside schedule)**
Losses:	**10 (6 inside schedule), 10 draws, 16 No Decisions and 1 No Contest**
Champ. record:	**5 wins, 1 draw, 1 defeat**
Titles:	**World heavyweight champion, 1908–15**

Left: Johnson's preference for white women made him the most hated man in America and – if his own story is true – cost him the championship.

He retained the title against white favourites like Stanley Ketchel, the middleweight champion who floored him in the 12th before being knocked out by the next punch, and former champion James J. Jeffries, who came out of retirement with the ringing exhortation from novelist Jack London to 'wipe the smile off the nigger's face'. It was bad enough that Johnson could beat all the white men, but when he flaunted a succession of white wives and mistresses, the Establishment was outraged.

He was prosecuted under the Mann Act, charged with transporting a woman across state lines for immoral purposes, and given a jail term. He fled to Europe and continued to box there, until (according to his version) he worked out a deal whereby the jail sentence would be quashed in return for him taking a dive against the white challenger Jess Willard in Havana in April 1915. Willard duly knocked him out in the 26th round, but refused to believe that his victory had been prearranged. 'If Johnson was going to take a dive, I wish he'd have done it sooner', Willard commented. 'It was hotter'n Hell out there.'

Johnson returned to America, where he served his sentence. He boxed sporadically until 1928, and was killed in a car crash on 10 June 1946.

Top: The first round of Johnson's final defence, against Willard in April 1915.

Inset: Traffic-stopper – Johnson is mobbed by Londoners in Fleet Street in 1911.

SONNY LISTON

CHARLES 'SONNY' LISTON managed only one successful defence of the world title. This ought to consign him to the second division of heavyweight champions, yet had justice been done, and he had been given a title shot when he first merited it, he would have reigned for four or five years. It is inconceivable that either the small and vulnerable Floyd Patterson or Ingemar Johansson, the Swede who briefly dethroned him in 1959, could have stood up to Liston's powerful jabs and concussive hooks. Muhammad Ali – Cassius Clay, as he then was – had the style to beat him, but Liston was an old man in boxing terms when he lost the championship to the youngster in February 1964.

No one knew for certain quite how old Liston was, because birth certificates were not issued for black children from the backwoods of Arkansas, where Liston was born into a family of 25 children. He claimed 8 May 1932 as his birth date, but it could never be verified and there were strong suggestions that he may have been anything up to ten years older.

The family moved to St. Louis when he was a boy, and he quickly found trouble. He was in an adult jail at fifteen, doing time for armed robbery, and was encouraged to take up boxing by a Catholic chaplain. There was no fairy-tale reformation, though: he continued to associate with gangsters and organized crime figures and did occasional jobs for them, including strike-breaking. His reputation quickly grew in the ring, with only one loss (to Marty Marshall, whom he later beat twice) in his first fifteen fights.

More problems with the law kept him out of the ring for almost two years between March 1956 and January 1958, but when he returned to action he rocketed up the rankings with a string of spectacular wins over men like Cleveland Williams (twice), Nino Valdes, Mike DeJohn, Zora Folley and Roy Harris. Eddie Machen, the craftiest heavyweight of the period, took him the full twelve

FORM LINE

Born:	**8 May 1932, St Francis, Arkansas**
Height:	**6 ft 1 in**
Weight:	**198–226 lb**
Pro debut:	**2 September 1953, St Louis; Don Smith, won, ref stopped fight Round 1**
Last fight:	**29 June 1970, Jersey City; Chuck Wepner, won, ref stopped fight Round 10**
Total fights:	**54**
Wins:	**50 (39 inside schedule)**
Losses:	**Four (three inside schedule)**
Champ. record:	**2 wins, 2 defeats**
Titles:	**World heavyweight champion, 1962–4**

Liston's glare alone was often enough to demoralize opponents: he was the most intimidating heavyweight in the business for years before becoming champion.

rounds but with that victory, in September 1960, the last obstacle between him and a title fight had been overcome.

But Cus D'Amato, who managed champion Floyd Patterson, preferred to keep his man occupied with a three-fight series against Johansson rather than face certain defeat by Liston, and it was not until Patterson broke with D'Amato and made the match himself that Liston's chance arrived, on 25 September 1962. Liston destroyed him in two minutes four seconds, and took six seconds longer to win the rematch.

He seemed set for a long reign, but Cassius Clay baffled and bewildered him into retirement after six rounds. Liston claimed to have damaged his shoulder, but in truth had been demoralized and humiliated.

There was worse to come, as Clay knocked him out in the first round in the return fight in May 1965, with a punch that scarcely anyone saw. Liston stayed out of the ring for two years, then made a moderately successful comeback that saw him lose only once in sixteen fights. Six months after his last fight, a 10th round stoppage of Chuck Wepner, the former champion was found dead on 30 December 1970 at his Las Vegas home, the victim of an apparent drugs overdose. The exact date of his death, like that of his birth, could not be determined.

Above: Eddie Machen, a crafty performer, frustrated Liston for 12 rounds at Seattle in 1960 but Liston's powerful jab carried him to victory.

Left: Sonny pounds the bag in preparation for his first fight with Floyd Patterson in Chicago in 1962.

JOE LOUIS

JOE LOUIS had to overcome more than just his heavyweight contemporaries to become world champion: he had first to break down the racial barriers that the white establishment had put in place to prevent any repetition of the Jack Johnson episode. The Johnson experience ensured that it would be twenty years before another black man would be given a chance to become champion: Louis ensured that, after him, colour would never again be a consideration. That is his legacy, to his country as well as his sport, and it is why he was buried in Arlington National Cemetery, which America reserves for its heroes.

Yet the Government which so honoured him in death had treated him shabbily in life, pursuing him for years for spiralling tax bills that mounted into absurd totals before President Kennedy wrote them off as a belated gesture of thanks for what he had done to improve race relations. By the fiery standards of today, Louis can seem almost servile in his attitudes, but he must be judged against the backdrop of his time. His management, who (unusually) were also black, worked hard to construct a public image of Louis as an agreeable, home-loving, non-threatening black man, distancing him as far as possible from the raucous, aggressive posturing of Johnson. Louis was not even allowed to be photographed with a white woman, let alone date one, and his every public statement was carefully scripted and rehearsed.

It worked, although the image-moulders were helped by the fact that Louis was also a sensationally good fighter whose stunning performances in the ring made his colour an irrelevance. Within eighteen months of his pro debut in July 1934, he had destroyed former champions Primo Carnera in six rounds and Max Baer in four, but then another ex-champ, Max Schmeling of Germany, slowed his progress when he knocked Louis out in twelve rounds.

Louis put it down to experience, and two months later hammered yet another former champion, Jack Sharkey, to defeat in three rounds. A year later, he was champion – but at a price. James J. Braddock, the wily old campaigner who held the title, agreed to give Louis his chance in return for a guaranteed $300,000 plus a percentage of Louis's earnings for the next ten years. That could have served as an inducement for Braddock to take the easy

FORM LINE

Born:	**13 May 1914, Lafayette, Alabama**
Height:	**6 ft $1^3/_4$ in**
Weight:	**188–218 lb**
Pro debut:	**4 July 1934, Chicago; Jack Kracken, won, ref stopped fight Round 1**
Last fight:	**26 October 1951, New York; Rocky Marciano, lost, KO Round 8**
Total fights:	**66**
Wins:	**63 (49 inside schedule)**
Losses:	**3 (2 inside schedule)**
Champ. record:	**26 wins, 1 defeat**
Titles:	**World heavyweight champion, 1937–49**

The Brown Bomber – at his peak, Louis was arguably the greatest of them all.

way out, but instead he floored Louis in the first round and battled with moving courage before Louis finished him in the eighth.

It was the start of a reign that has never been equalled. He retained the title an astonishing 25 times, and that total would doubtless have been higher if the Second World War had not coincided with his peak years. Louis gave everyone a chance, whether they were leading contenders or Bums Of The Month, and only two – Billy Conn and Jersey Joe Walcott – came close to beating him. He retired in 1949 as undefeated champion, but his tax problems made a comeback inevitable.

Ezzard Charles beat him in 1950 for the NBA title, and although he won his next nine fights against decent opposition, he quit for good after Rocky Marciano knocked him out in 1951. His later years were ravaged by drugs and illness, but his popularity was undiminished until his death on 12 April 1981.

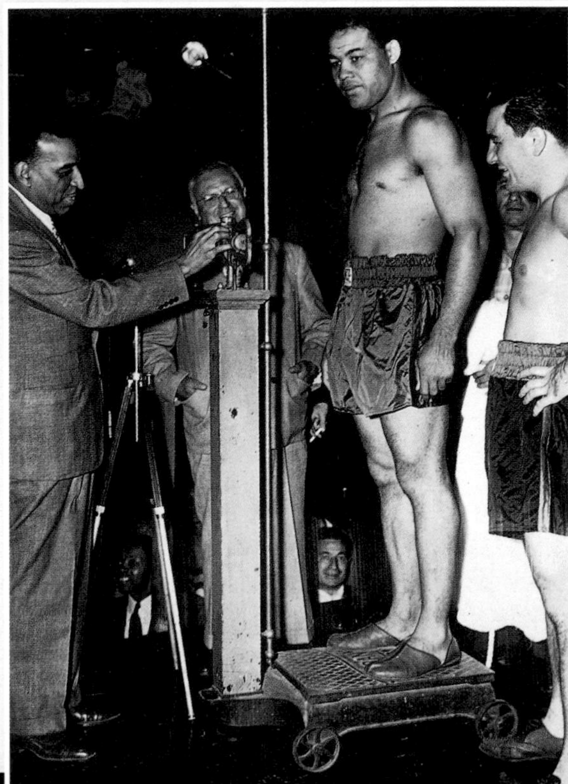

Left: Louis weighs in for a defence against Tami Mauriello at Yankee Stadium on 19 September 1946: Mauriello was flattened in the first round.

Below: The battered and bloody Lee Savold goes down and out in the sixth round as Louis's comeback rolls along in 1951.

ROCKY MARCIANO

MAN OR machine, it made no difference to Rocky Marciano. He faced 49 opponents in the ring and beat them all, 43 by knockout or stoppage, and when a computer paired him in a 'dream fight' with Muhammad Ali just weeks before his death in a plane crash on 31 August 1969, he won that one as well. Of course, human factors had much to do with the computer's decision, not least the fact that Ali's unpopularity in America was then at its height because of his opposition to the Vietnam War and his refusal to join the Army, while there was a parallel nostalgia for the simpler, less sophisticated era represented by Marciano. It is highly unlikely that the short and crude Marciano could really have beaten the quicksilver genius of Ali, but it is a stone-cold certainty that he would have given him Hell.

FORM LINE

Born:	**1 September 1923, Brockton, Massachusetts**
Height:	**5ft 10$^{1/4}$ in**
Weight:	**178–192 lb**
Pro debut:	**17 March 1947, Holyoke, Mass.; Lee Epperson, won, KO Round 3**
Last fight:	**21 September 1955, New York; Archie Moore, won, KO Round 9**
Total fights:	**49**
Wins:	**49 (43 inside schedule)**
Losses:	**0**
Champ. record:	**7 wins, no defeats**
Titles:	**World heavyweight champion, 1952–6**

Marciano – real name Marchegiano – was a fierce competitor, a warrior who, even in his most desperate moments, simply refused to recognize the possibility of defeat. He came late to boxing, not taking it up until he was 23, and he never mastered more than the rudiments of what in his case could never be called the 'Sweet Science'. But what he lacked in subtlety was more than compensated for by his raw determination and immense natural physical strength. He was the shortest of all the modern heavyweight champions, yet like Mike Tyson he possessed disproportionate punching power.

His trainer Charley Goldman, an old-time bantamweight veteran of 300 fights, was shrewd enough to work on Marciano's strengths rather than his flaws, accepting that he would never be a natural boxer. Instead of baffling him with complex moves, he taught him to channel his power into short hooks and uppercuts, and the results were dramatic as he flattened all eleven opponents in his first full year as a pro, 1948.

Wins over Roland LaStarza, Rex Layne, Freddie Beshore, Harry Matthews and the faded Joe Louis earned him a shot at Jersey Joe Walcott's world title in Philadelphia on 23 September 1952, but the ancient Walcott almost spoilt the script by flooring him in the

Marciano was well-named: the Rock was truly indestructible in the ring.

Above: Roland LaStarza (right) had given Rocky a tough time in their first meeting, but he was crushed in this rematch in 1953.

Left: Clever Ezzard Charles lasted the full fifteen with Marciano in a classic encounter in 1954.

first round. Walcott boxed a superb tactical fight, and the challenger was outmanoeuvred in round after round before, in the 13th, Marciano won the title with the hardest single punch of his career.

Walcott succumbed in the first round of their rematch, and his old rival Roland LaStarza lasted into the 11th round of his title challenge in 1953.

Former champion Ezzard Charles proved Marciano's toughest opponent. He had two classic encounters with Marciano in 1954, losing the first on points and splitting Marciano's nose almost in half in the return before, yet again, Rocky salvaged a lost cause with one punch. Marciano retained the title twice more, against England's Don Cockell and light-heavyweight champion Archie Moore, before unexpectedly retiring on 27 April 1956. He had fallen out with his manager Al Weill, and had wearied of the sacrifices and rigours of training. He resisted all offers to come back, but retained enough competitor's pride to shed more than 40 lb for the filming of his 'fight' with Ali.

MIKE TYSON

MIKE TYSON was born for trouble, and with hindsight the only surprising aspect of his self-destruction was that it took so long to happen. Yet what a fighter he was in his brief but glorious prime. *That* Mike Tyson rates with the authentic giants of the division, and had he been able to maintain the focus and dedication he showed in the first few years of his meteoric professional career, his potential was boundless.

Jim Jacobs, the former handball champion who co-managed him in those early days, used to say only half-jokingly that the master plan was for Tyson to clean up in the division, retire when he had fought himself out of marketable competition, stay away for five or six years to allow a new generation of contenders to emerge, and then come out of retirement and repeat the whole cycle. He could have done it, too, had his life turned out differently.

But the seeds of self-destruction were always there, in his fatherless, ghetto upbringing and in the extraordinary hot-house atmosphere to which he was subjected when his possibilities as a boxer were first spotted in his early teens. He was in reform school at the time, but was signed out to the care of the eccentric but brilliant trainer Cus D'Amato, who saw in him the raw material from which to mould a heavyweight champion. D'Amato was backed financially by Jim Jacobs and his partner Bill Cayton, and when D'Amato became too infirm to work with the youngster he delegated the job to his protégé Kevin Rooney.

Tyson's adolescence was filled with boxing, boxing, boxing to the exclusion of virtually everything else. Between them, his mentors produced a near-perfect fighting machine, but along the way they forgot that he was also a troubled young boy as much in need of emotional and spiritual guidance as coaching in the best way to throw a left hook. They developed the machine but ignored the man, and the consequences for Tyson would eventually be devastating.

Tyson ripped through the mediocre competition the heavyweight division offered in the mid-1980s, stopping Trevor Berbick for the WBC title in November 1986, and 27 months after his debut in March 1985 he unified the title for the first time in nine years. He was at his peak in 1988, when he destroyed Larry Holmes, Tony Tubbs and Mike Spinks, but his life was collapsing into chaos after the unexpected death of Jacobs, his estrangement from Cayton, and a messy divorce from

FORM LINE

Born:	**30 June 1966, Brooklyn, New York**
Height:	**5 ft 11 in**
Weight:	**214-222 lb**
Pro debut:	**6 March 1985, New York; Hector Mercedes, won, ref stopped fight Round 1**
Last fight:	**10 November 1996, Las Vegas; Evander Holyfield, lost, ref stopped fight Round 11**
Total fights:	**47**
Wins:	**45 (39 insideschedule)**
Losses:	**2 (both inside schedule)**
Champ. record:	**12 wins, 2 defeats**
Titles:	**Twice world heavyweight champion (1986-90, 1996)**

Ready to rumble – Tyson paces the ring before his comeback against Peter McNeeley in 1995.

Above: Frank Bruno survived this first-round knockdown to take Tyson into the fifth round in Las Vegas in 1989.

Right: Razor Ruddock is knocked off balance by Tyson's unorthodox left in their first fight in 1991.

actress Robin Givens, a gold-digger who gave her finest performance at the wedding ceremony.

Without Rooney's training discipline and corner expertise, Tyson floundered to shocking defeat against the rank outsider James 'Buster' Douglas in February 1990. He rebuilt with four wins, including two over the dangerous Razor Ruddock, but then was jailed for six years for raping a contestant in a beauty pageant. After his release in 1995 he quickly won the WBC and WBA versions of the title, but relinquished the WBC belt and then suffered a crushing setback when veteran Evander Holyfield stopped him for the WBA title. His comeback had been a financial bonanza, grossing him anything up to $100m, but the Holyfield defeat ensured that Iron Mike would never again hold the same terror for future opponents.

Chapter 4

Classic Fights

GREAT fights can happen in obscure halls, between boxers whose fame will never extend beyond their hometown. But to be truly memorable, there has to be a championship involved – and when two superb fighters clash with the title on the line on a night when they each hit their career peak, the result is sublime, an occasion and an atmosphere as close to perfection as sport has to offer. Here are a few of the best. . . .

R O U N D

Ray Leonard and Roberto Duran shared one of the ring's great rivalries, but when they met for the third time Leonard (right) was clearly the master.

WILLIE PEP VS SANDY SADDLER

World featherweight title, New York, 11 February 1949

THE SHEER statistics of Willie Pep's career are awe-inspiring. He turned pro at 17, won 62 in a row before lightweight champion Sammy Angott outpointed him, and then won another 73 in succession. In November 1942 he became the youngest featherweight champion for 40 years by beating Chalky Wright for the New York version, and had it not been for the Second World War would have extended that phenomenal winning run even further. The War restricted him to three defences, but he unified the title in June 1947 and retained it twice more before, in a huge upset, Sandy Saddler knocked him out in four rounds in October 1948.

Saddler, too, had been extra-ordinarily busy – he had fought 93 times in four and a half years when he took Pep's crown, but had lost six times along the way. There was bad blood between them, with Saddler – a notoriously dirty fighter – fouling Pep repeatedly but finding that Willie, for all his technical brilliance, was no angel himself. The New York State Athletic Commissioner was so concerned about the possibility of a dirty fight, and the rumours that the result of the first meeting between the two fighters had been fixed, that he warned them he would be extra-vigiliant in following the action that night in Madison Square Garden. As it happened, he had nothing to worry about. Pep was determined to regain his title and his reputation as a master-boxer, and he landed his jab 37 times in Saddler's face in the first round alone. It took the champion four rounds to land a worthwhile punch, to Pep's body, but by the fifth Pep was cut under the left eye as Saddler's dangerous rights began to find their mark.

> **"It took the champion four rounds to land a worthwhile punch, to Pep's body, but by the fifth Pep was cut under the left eye as Saddler's dangerous rights began to find their mark. Pep began to slow from the seventh and was cut again, but his jab kept ramming into Saddler's face and earning points."**

Pep began to slow from the seventh and was cut again, but his jab kept ramming into Saddler's face and earning points. Saddler was missing more than he landed, which always drains a man's strength, and Pep seemed to get his second wind and danced around him, landing jab after jab and counter-attacking suddenly from unexpected angles. Saddler was confused and bewildered, but he never stopped trying for the big right that could save his title. He almost managed it in the final round, but Pep held on and smothered until the crisis had past. He took a deserved, unanimous verdict, but needed eight stitches to close the cuts on his battered face.

They would fight twice more, with Saddler winning both inside the distance – but on this night and this performance, Pep reserved his place with the legends.

Sandy Saddler's attempted block is marginally too late as the bloodied Willie Pep lands a crashing right in their 1949 epic.

CLASSIC FIGHTS

CARMEN BASILIO

VS

SUGAR RAY ROBINSON

World middleweight title, New York, 23 September 1957

CARMEN BASILIO'S lined and weathered face told its own story of poverty, deprivation, hard work and hammerings. The one-time onion farmer from Canastota in upstate New York had fought his way through the preliminary ranks to become world welterweight champion at the second attempt in 1955, and had lost and regained it by the time he challenged the fabulous Sugar Ray Robinson for the middleweight title in Yankee Stadium, New York. He was a ten-year veteran with 70 fights behind him, of which he had lost twelve and drawn seven.

That scarcely compared to Robinson's glittering record of 148 fights with just five defeats, two draws and one No Contest. Ray, the former undefeated welterweight champion, was in his fourth reign as middleweight champion, and at the age of 37 showed no sign of weakening. He had a six-pounds weight advantage (160 to 154) and started a clear favourite over the short, stumpy Basilio.

He looked the part in the early exchanges, snapping jabs into Basilio's face even though the challenger fought out of a crouching stance which emphasized the five-inch height disparity. Basilio knew that he had to get past the jab to be effective, but whenever he did Robinson invariably tied him up. In the fourth, a right opened a cut over Basilio's left eye, but he kept doggedly advancing and, by the fifth, was starting to pin Robinson on the ropes and hammer his body.

Robinson had a good sixth, but from the seventh onwards Basilio's persistent attacks had him on the retreat and looking anxious. The rugged challenger consistently outfought the veteran through to the 11th, but then Robinson, always the supreme competitor, switched to the offensive and battered Basilio for the first two minutes of the round before the challenger came back strongly in the final minute.

It looked as though the champion must fall, but instead he survived and, miraculously, turned the fight his way again in the 12th with a blistering attack that had Basilio reeling. Somehow the New Yorker made it through the round, and had to soak up more punishment in the next as well. But it was Robinson's Last Hurrah: he was spent, and Basilio dictated the pace in the final two rounds as the weary Robinson, feeling every day of his 37 years, stayed out of trouble.

As they awaited the verdict, Basilio dropped to one knee in prayer. It was a close call: a split decision, 2-1 in Basilio's favour. He never won another title fight. Six months later, Robinson took revenge in a fight almost as thrilling as that first, unforgettable encounter.

"Ray, the former undefeated welterweight champion, was in his fourth reign as middleweight champion, and at the age of 37 showed no sign of weakening. He had a six-pounds weight advantage (160 to 154) and started a clear favourite over the short, stumpy Basilio."

The strain of a gruelling battle is evident on both men as Basilio (right) swarms into the attack in the closing stages of their first fight.

JOE FRAZIER

VS

MUHAMMAD ALI

World heavyweight title, New York, 8 March 1971

GREAT champions need great opponents, and Joe Frazier and Muhammad Ali were the perfect pair. Theirs was a match made in Heaven, bringing together two undefeated heavyweight champions who were also bitter personal as well as professional rivals. It was fitting they should begin their historic three-fight series in Madison Square Garden, since the New York venue (in its several incarnations) was boxing's spiritual home and these were two of the game's finest exponents. Ali was undefeated in 31 fights, but his refusal to join the Army had cost him his title and three and a half of his peak career years. Frazier, who had snapped up the vacant title, had won all 26 fights, 23 inside schedule.

Ali started well, winning the first few rounds by stabbing quick lefts into Frazier's face and tying up the champion at close quarters, clowning and playing to the gallery as he shook his head in derision at Frazier's efforts. But by the third, significantly, Smokin' Joe had succeeded in bulling past the jab and was punishing Ali to the body, hacking and ripping in ferocious hooks. Frazier took the fourth as well, but Ali's long-range boxing edged him ahead in the middle rounds, and Frazier had to prove his toughness by absorbing some solid head punches too.

The rivals were beautifully matched, the contrast between Ali's smooth skills and Frazier's swarming, bulling aggression providing an absorbing spectacle. But Ali was finding it hard to maintain the ferocious pace, while Frazier, who had been fighting regularly during Ali's enforced layoff, was relishing it. Going into the 11th it was still possible for Ali to win, although he trailed on the cards of two of the three judges. Early in the round, Ali leaned back on the ropes to make Frazier miss, as he had done so often already, but this time a left hook caught him flush and for the rest of the round he was in such desperate trouble that the referee, Arthur Mercante, checked on his condition in the corner during the interval before the 12th.

From then on, it was Frazier's fight, even though Ali won the 14th on two cards with a final, all-or-nothing rally. Any lingering doubts evaporated in the first minute of the last round, when a wide, arcing left hook dumped Ali on his back, legs in the air. He got up to take the eight count, his jaw grotesquely swollen, and defied all Joe's attempts to put him down again. At the final bell, Frazier laughed in his face. He'd won this time, unanimously, but Ali's day would come.

> **"The rivals were beautifully matched, the contrast between Ali's smooth skills and Frazier's swarming, bulling aggression providing an absorbing spectacle."**

Ali scored well with jabs in the opening rounds (left), but Frazier's relentless pressure ground him down (right) and (top) a sweeping left hook in the 15th round clinched the win for Smokin' Joe.

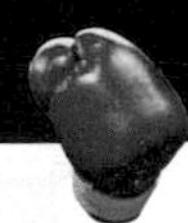

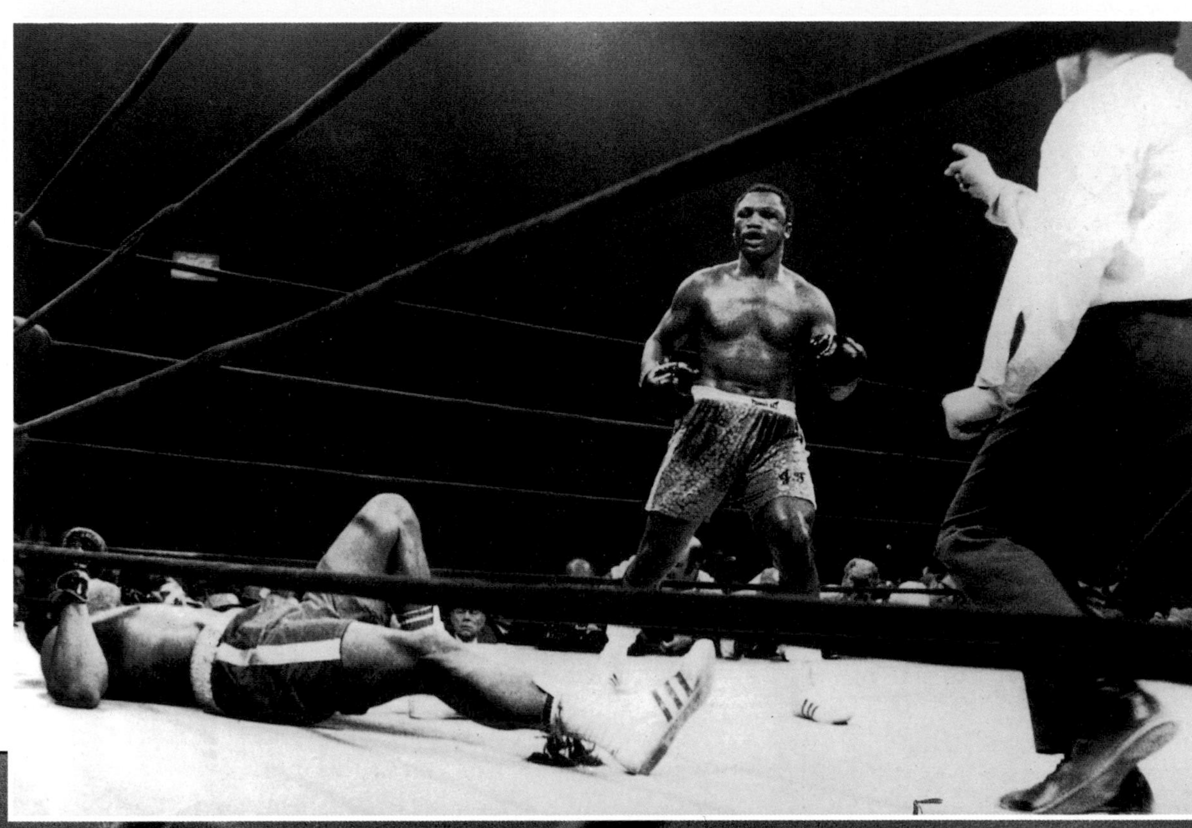

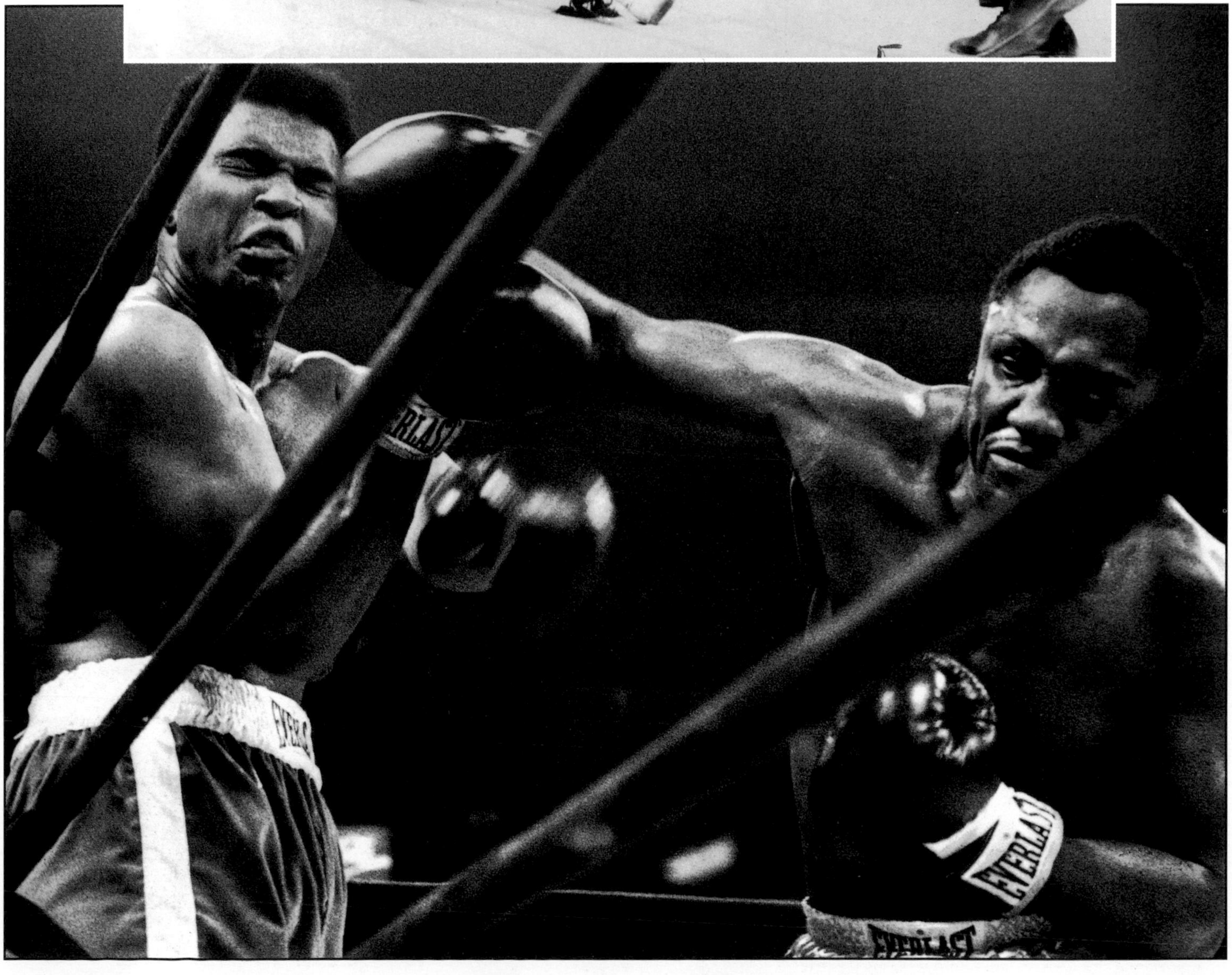

MUHAMMAD ALI

VS

JOE FRAZIER

World heavyweight title, Manila, 1 October 1975

AFTER TWO epic clashes with a win apiece, Muhammad Ali and Joe Frazier had unfinished business. Joe floored and outpointed him first time around in 1971, and three years later Ali edged him out in a twelve-rounds thriller for the North American Boxing Federation title. By the time they met in the decider, in October 1975, both were on the way down. Frazier's style meant that his would always be a short and explosive career, but for Ali the decline was more gradual. Even so, their third meeting produced one of the most relentlessly thrilling championships of all time and all weights, almost as if they each realized that this would be the fight, above all their others, by which history would judge and remember them.

It was promoted by Don King, then making his way as a big-time operator, and he billed it as the 'Thrilla In Manila'. For once, the action matched the hype and the 25,000 crowd, who caused a three-hour traffic jam around the stadium, witnessed the last great performances of two outstanding champions.

Ali discarded his familiar dancing routine in favour of red-blooded action, planting himself in mid-ring and hammering the stocky Frazier with solid hooks. None made any significant impression on the challenger, though: he gritted his teeth and kept marching forward, firing his own destructive left hooks like a clockwork toy. From the fourth to the sixth, Frazier began to have more success as he kept Ali pinned on the ropes for long spells, but from the seventh Ali got on his toes and moved away from the ever-advancing Philadelphian, spearing him with jabs and lashing right-hand counters. But Frazier, impassive, chugged away and whenever he got close enough, buried his head on Ali's shoulder and ripped hooks to the body.

The champion made his big effort in the 12th as Frazier, his face swollen and his left eye closing, was driven back under a barrage of blows, particularly from Ali's right as Ali took full advantage of his opponent's impaired vision. The 13th was a nightmare for the exhausted Frazier, but he was too much a warrior to quit. Ali, too, was flagging and the realization that the champion was in almost as bad shape as himself kept Frazier going in the 14th. But he had nothing left, and his compassionate trainer Eddie Futch would not let him take another punch.

'Sit down, son, it's all over', he told his beaten charge at the end of the round. 'But nobody will ever forget what you did here today.'

"The champion made his big effort in the 12th as Frazier, his face swollen and his left eye closing, was driven back under a barrage of blows as Ali took full advantage of his opponent's impaired vision."

Frazier's battered face (above) tells its own story, while (right) Ali shows how his opponent got to look that way.

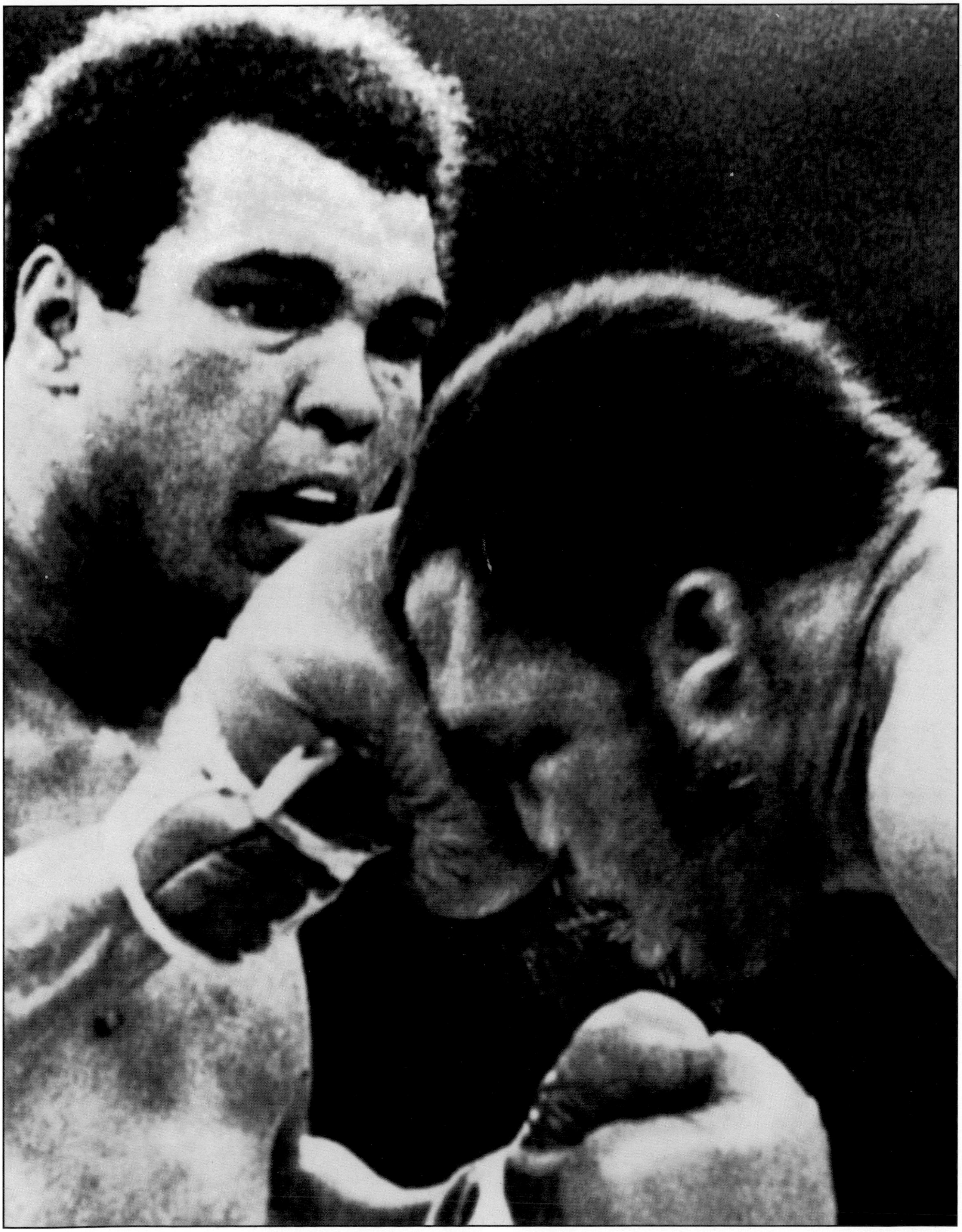

CLASSIC FIGHTS

ROBERTO DURAN

 VS 

SUGAR RAY LEONARD

WBC welterweight title, Montreal, 20 June 1980

IT IS RARE to see a fighter grow and prove himself in defeat, but that is what Sugar Ray Leonard did the night Roberto Duran took his WBC welterweight title in Montreal. In a sense, the loss was the making of Leonard, because it was in the way he fought Duran that he convinced himself, and the rest of us, that he was not just a pretty boxer but a hard and rugged competitor who could, as they say in London, do it on the cobbles as well as in the ring. Any man who could stand head-to-head with Roberto Duran, as he did unflinchingly, demanded respect.

At that time, the fearsome Panamanian was at his peak. He had won 70 of his 71 fights, been lightweight champion for nine years, and had fought himself out of competition in his own division when he decided to 'move up' in search of new challenges. They didn't come any more challenging than Leonard, the biggest star in American boxing. The former Olympic champion had earned a million dollars as challenger when he took the title from Wilfred Benitez in November 1979, and looked chillingly good in dispatching the Englishman Dave Green with one left hook in the fourth round of his first defence.

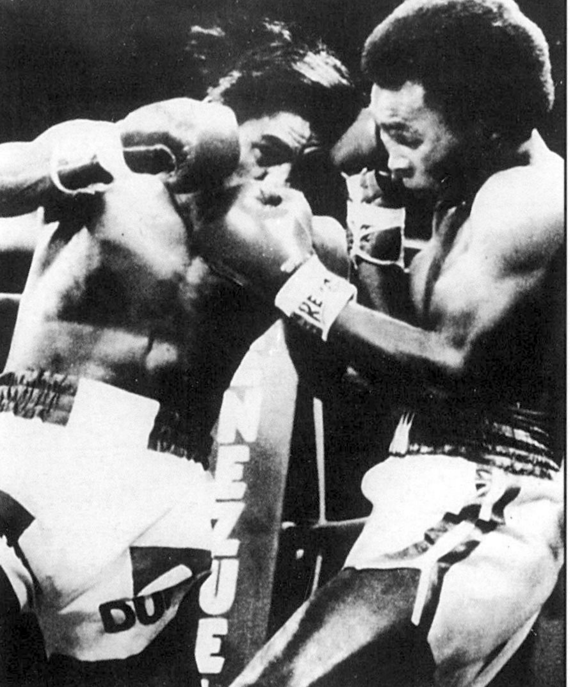

He could have outboxed Duran, as he proved decisively in their two subsequent meetings, but instead he decided to take him on at his own game and out-macho the ultimate macho man. It made for magnificent entertainment, but as a fight strategy it was crazy. Duran wasn't complaining, though, especially as referee Carlos Padilla (normally a fussy official) decided early on to let them get as rough as they liked at close quarters without interference from him. This was Duran's kind of fight, and he revelled in it.

Leonard scored constantly with crisp and classy punches, but the sheer volume of blows from Duran kept him in front. There were no knockdowns, just hard and unremitting action as two proud men refused to concede an inch of ground. It was rough and nasty, not a sight for the faint-hearted, but even though he was losing Leonard was growing in stature by the moment as he proved he had a warrior's spirit to match Duran's.

When the final bell sounded, there was no token embrace from Duran: he laughed in exultation, and ignored Leonard's outstretched glove as he walked to the ropes to claim victory even before the judges made it official with a unanimous verdict in his favour. Five months later, on the infamous night when Duran shouted 'No Mas' and quit in the eighth round, it was a different story. Leonard had lost the fight, but he would win the war.

"There were no knockdowns, just hard and unremitting action as two proud men refused to concede an inch of ground. It was rough and nasty, not a sight for the faint-hearted."

Above: Forged in the furnace – Leonard, under more pressure than he had ever experienced, proved his worth by fighting on Duran's terms.

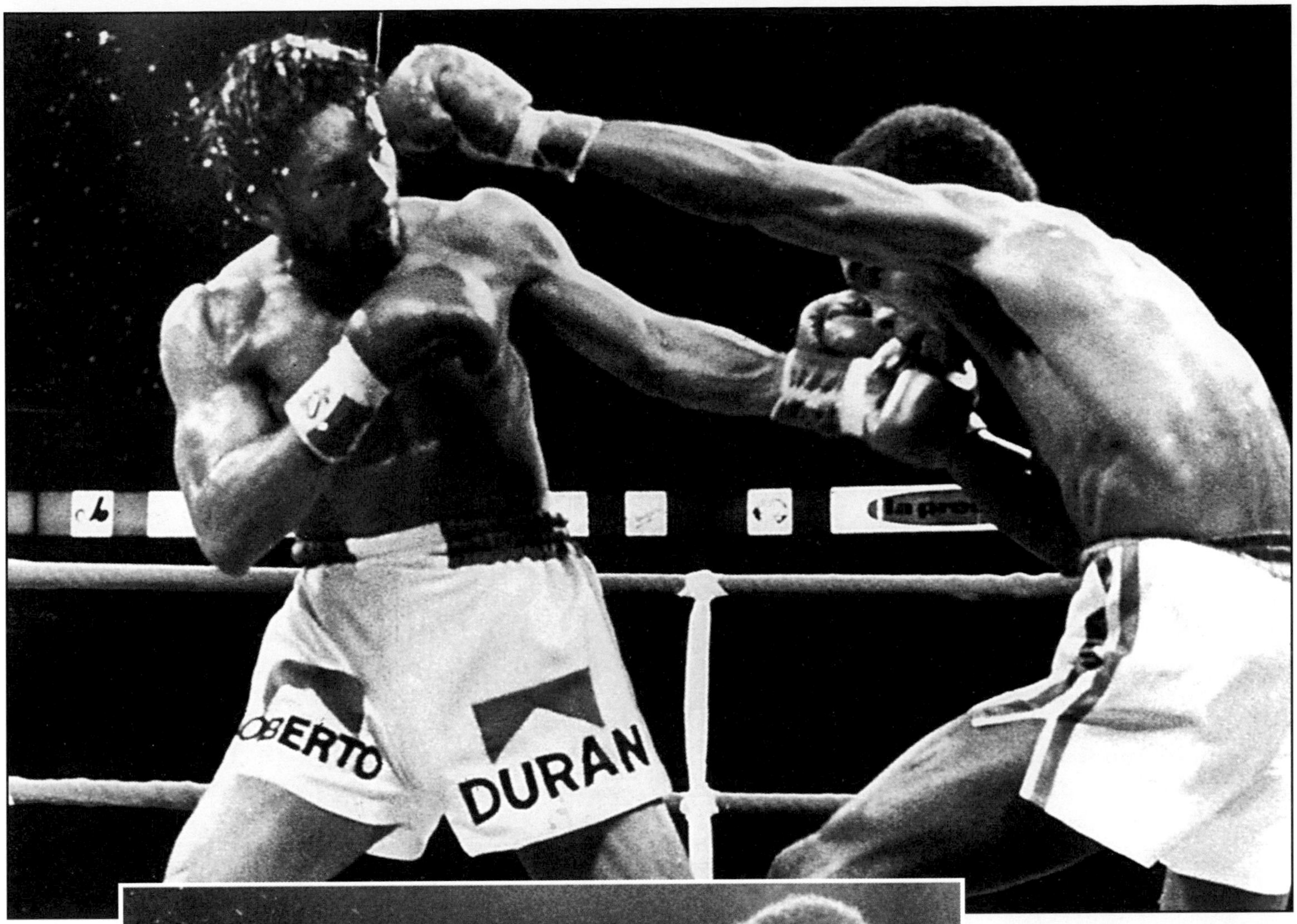

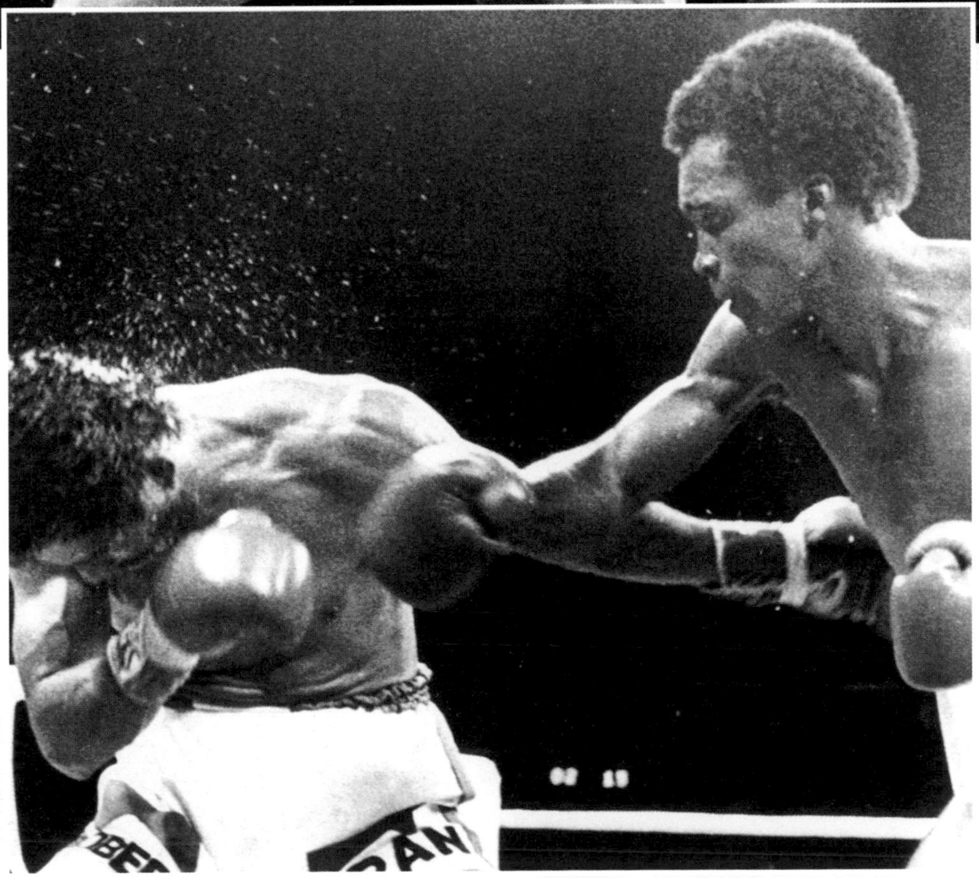

Above and left: Even with defeat looming, Leonard's precision and accuracy were impeccable – but he could never land solidly enough to stop Duran's charge.

MARVIN HAGLER

VS

THOMAS HEARNS

World middleweight title, Las Vegas, 15 April 1985

WHEN **Marvin Hagler faced** Thomas Hearns at Caesars Palace, Las Vegas, in April 1985, there was much more at stake than merely the middleweight championship of the world. There was ego and pride, fired by the genuine, deep-seated animosity between two men universally acknowledged to be among the best pound-for-pound in the business – not to mention the biggest purse either would earn. The fight had taken more than three years to make, and the fans' anticipation built as the insults and slurs flew back and forth, with each accusing the other of ducking him.

Hearns, the WBC light-middleweight champion, was expected to try to outbox the bigger man, but instead chose to go head-to-head with Hagler in an opening round that is still recalled, with awe, as the most explosive three minutes ever seen in a championship ring. There was no attempt on either side to jab; every punch was a vicious hook or uppercut, intended (in Hagler's favourite expression) to 'Destruct and Destroy'. Hearns was finally backed to the ropes, where for fully half a minute the men smashed punches at each other until suddenly, shockingly, Hagler was cut.

> **"Hagler ignored the blood as he hurled himself at the spindly challenger, but referee Richard Steele was keeping a close watch and when he called 'Stop boxing', it seemed the fight was over. 'Can you see him?', Steele asked. 'I'm not missing him, am I?' was Hagler's laconic reply, showing extreme self-possession in the moment of supreme crisis."**

Blood cascaded from a long, vertical gash on his forehead, and he brushed it angrily away with his glove before gathering himself for another assault, this time with an air of desperation as he realized the injury was too bad to sustain a long fight. Hearns rode out the storm, and drew fresh encouragement in the second round as another ugly cut split open under the champion's right eye. Hagler ignored the blood as he hurled himself at the spindly challenger, but referee Richard Steele was keeping a close watch and when he called 'Stop boxing', it seemed the fight was over.

'Can you see him?', Steele asked.

'I'm not missing him, am I?' was Hagler's laconic reply, showing extreme self-possession in the moment of supreme crisis. Steele waved them on, and imperceptibly at first but then clearly, the balance shifted as Hagler's precise southpaw blows began to break up an opponent who, having given his best, was now starting to suffer.

Hearns tried to rally in the third, but there was nothing left and a right hook sent him staggering back, spinning almost a full circle. Hagler sprinted after him, and three more rights – more clubs than hooks – spread-eagled the challenger. Drawing on his last reserves of strength and spirit, Hearns hauled himself upright – but Steele had seen enough, and wrapped his arms around the swaying, vacant-eyed loser.

Right: Hearns is still full of fight in round two (above), but Hagler's mighty right took everything out of him in the third (below).

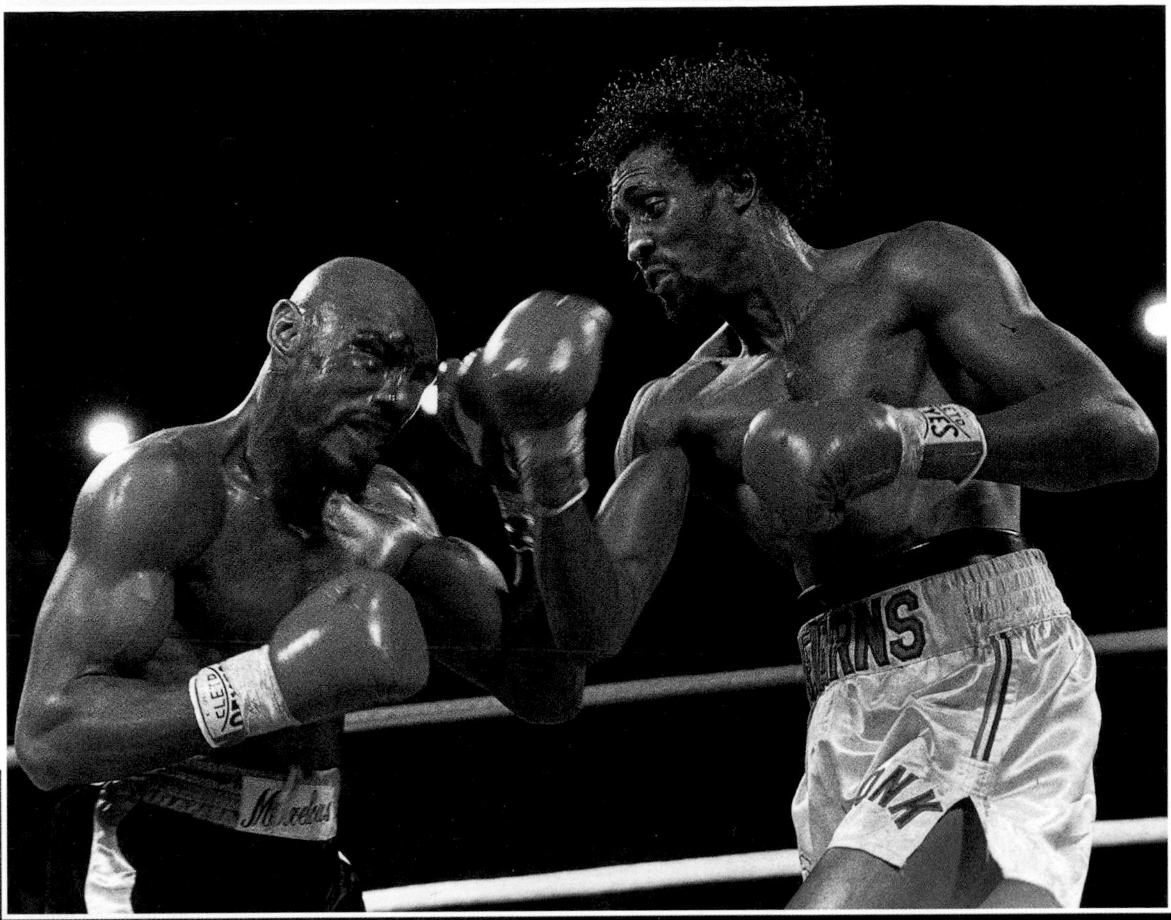

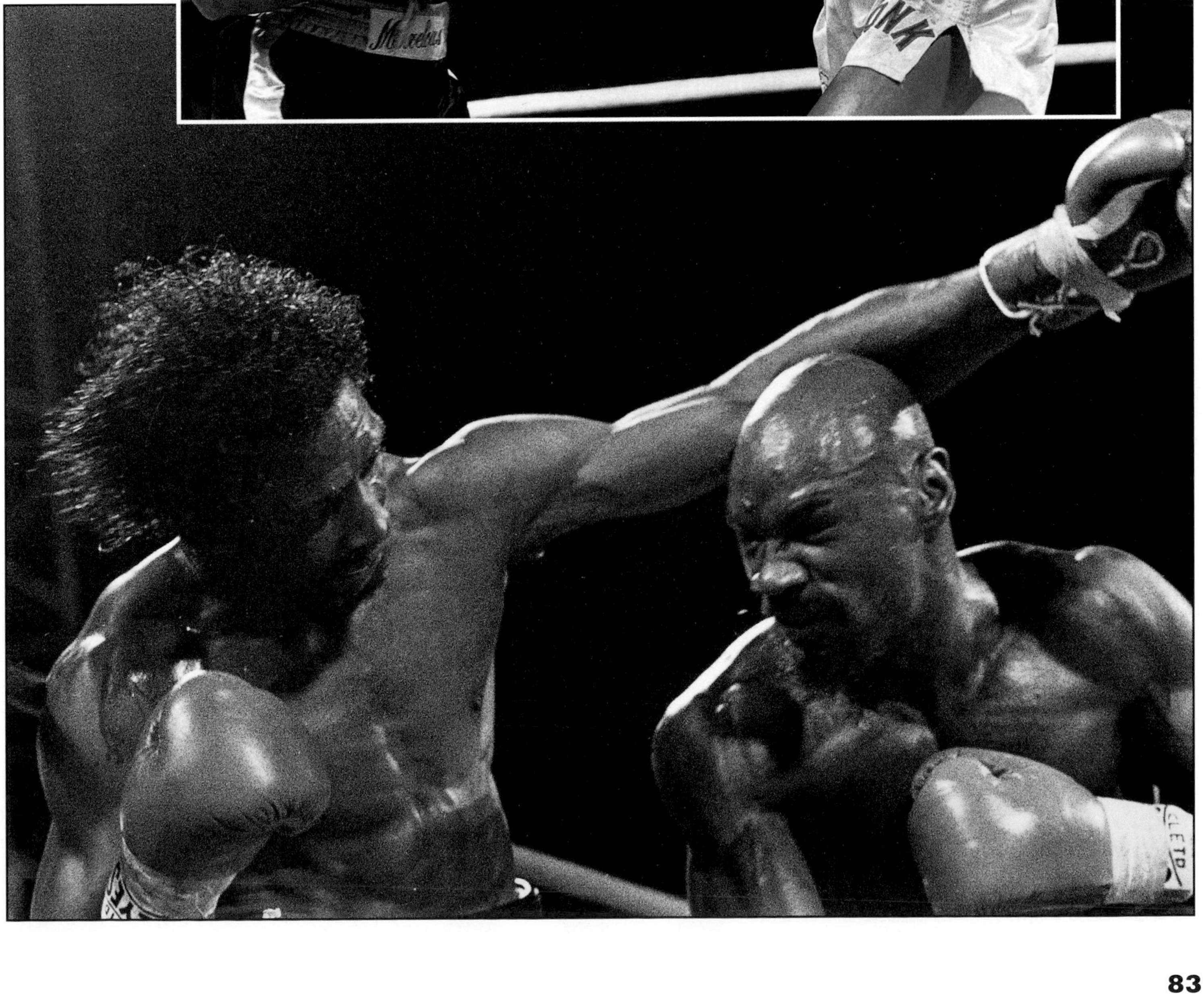

BARRY McGUIGAN

VS

EUSEBIO PEDROZA

WBA featherweight title, London, 8 June 1985

IT SEEMED that everyone wanted to be there when the charismatic Irishman Barry McGuigan challenged Eusebio Pedroza for the WBA featherweight title, but only 26,000 could squeeze into Queen's Park Rangers' compact stadium at Loftus Road, London. The rest had to be content with watching on television – and so many did so that the fight drew a bigger television audience than the FA Cup Final. It was easy to understand why, because the appeal of the dark-haired, fiery McGuigan transcended boxing. He was one of the most recognizible faces in the country, and a brilliant marketing campaign had projected him as a symbol of unity at a time when the Troubles were tearing Northern Ireland apart.

The fight would have been a major attraction whoever the opponent, but the fact that the champion was a superb craftsman making his twentieth defence rendered it irresistible. Pedroza was a globe-trotter who feared no one and went anywhere there was a payday to be earned. He had risked and retained his title in places as far apart as Papua New Guinea, Puerto Rico, Japan, America, Korea, Italy and Venezuela, so he had no qualms about coming to London to make another defence of his crown, even though he respected McGuigan enough to wring almost £1m out of promoter Barney Eastwood, who also managed the challenger.

The Panamanian was a master boxer, and he showed McGuigan the full range of his skills in the opening four rounds as he whipped in uppercuts and speared him with long left jabs. But the Irishman was always slow to build an attacking rhythm, and by the fifth he was beginning to make his presence felt with crunching left hooks to the lean champion's ribs. Body-punching was McGuigan's forte, but it was a perfect right to the head which dropped Pedroza in the seventh and turned the fight decisively McGuigan's way.

Pedroza rallied defiantly to win the eighth, but the challenger almost floored him again in the ninth and from then on it was a question of whether the old champ's heart would carry him through the full fifteen rounds. Pedroza had a reputation as a dirty fighter, but he boxed this time with flawless sportsmanship and skill. McGuigan, though, had the power and the enthusiasm of youth, and his surging aggression built a lead that Pedroza could never hope to overhaul. The spindly Panamanian was a punch from defeat in a punishing 13th round, but courage saw him through to the final bell. The verdict in the Irishman's favour after fifteen magnificent rounds was unanimous.

“Pedroza rallied defiantly to win the eighth, but the challenger almost floored him again in the ninth and from then on it was a question of whether the old champ's heart would carry him through the full fifteen rounds.”

Right: McGuigan took time to find the range in early exchanges (top), but almost stopped the classy Pedroza in the 13th (below).

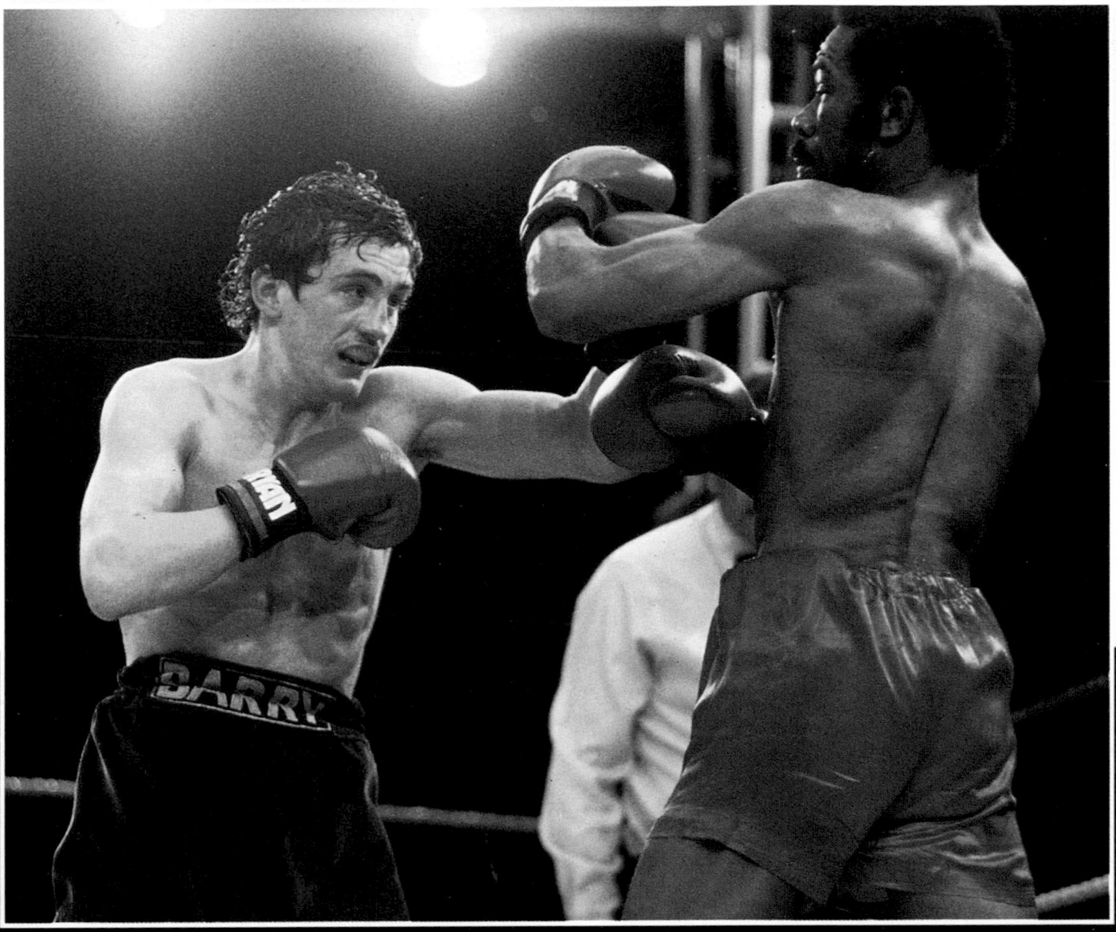

CLASSIC FIGHTS

JULIO CESAR CHAVEZ VS MELDRICK TAYLOR

WBC and IBF light-welterweight titles, Las Vegas, 17 March 1990

SOME fighters never know when they are beaten: that is what makes them champions. Julio Cesar Chavez, Mexico's greatest-ever boxer, had already proved himself a dozen times over, but the way in which he snatched victory from Meldrick Taylor in the dying seconds offered the final confirmation of his status as one of the game's immortals. Their meeting at the Las Vegas Hilton was a perfect match, a rare pairing of two undefeated champions in a unification bout. Chavez, the WBC light-welterweight champion, was unbeaten in 68 fights with 55 inside-schedule wins, while IBF champ Taylor had won 23 and drawn one. Taylor was a consummate boxer, while Chavez was the ultimate pressure fighter, a patient hunter in the ring who stalked his opponents and broke them up steadily with wicked hooks to the ribs.

The fight was billed as 'Thunder And Lightning', and the label summed up the contrasting styles wonderfully well. Taylor had been the Olympic featherweight gold medallist in 1984, and he boxed with a featherweight's speed in the first half of the twelve-rounder, whipping in clusters of hooks and picking off the plodding Mexican with accurate jabs. Chavez looked slow and one-paced, and the Philadelphian repeatedly beat him to the punch.

Even when Chavez managed to connect, he could only land single blows rather than the combinations that might have broken Taylor's rhythm. The large Mexican contingent in the crowd tried to get their man going, but Chavez seemed unable to increase his pace or change his tactics. As the rounds reeled off, Taylor's lead grew insurmountable: one judge gave him seven of the first eight rounds. A fierce exchange at the start of the ninth saw Chavez rocked by three left hooks, but he was as brave as ever and blasted back with short hooks.

Taylor took the 10th easily, and raised his arms in a victory salute as he got off the stool to start the 11th. He had the better of that round too, outpunching Chavez in some thrilling exchanges. Coming out for the final round, Taylor led by 108-101 and 107-102, with the third judge, inexplicably, having Chavez in front by 105-104. Taylor had only to survive the round to take a clear points win, but Chavez was not beaten yet. He started the round as if it was the first, ripping hooks at the tiring American and pressuring him relentlessly.

Finally, a heavy right rocked Taylor. He tried to hang on, but another right dropped him in a corner. He got up at five, badly dazed, and referee Richard Steele looked closely at him before signalling the end. The time was 2 minutes 58 seconds of the 12th round: Taylor was just two seconds from victory.

"The large Mexican contingent in the crowd tried to get their man going, but Chavez seemed unable to increase his pace or change his tactics. As the rounds reeled off, Taylor's lead grew insurmountable."

Right: It's not over until the final bell – outpunched for most of the fight, Chavez devastated Taylor with two rights seconds from the end to claim victory.

CLASSIC FIGHTS

NIGEL BENN

GERALD McCLELLAN

WBC super-middleweight title, London, 25 February 1995

THIS LOOKED like Mission Impossible for Nigel Benn, who was making the seventh and, most critics assumed, final defence of the WBC super-middleweight title he had won from Mauro Galvano in October 1992. The man in the other corner at the London Arena in Millwall, East London, Gerald McClellan from Detroit, had a fair claim to being the most feared fighter in the world, with an extraordinary record of 31 wins in 33 fights, 29 inside the distance and 20 in the first round. Benn had made a similar start to his career, winning his first 22 inside schedule with eleven in the opening round, but the difference was that McClellan continued to win quickly at the very highest level. He lifted the WBO middleweight title in the first round, stopped the fearsome Julian Jackson in a five-round thriller for the WBC version, and retained it three times, all inside a round.

He looked like adding Benn to the list when he battered him through the ropes and onto the ring apron in the first minute of the fight. The capacity 12,000 crowd were almost as stunned as Benn. Somehow the dazed champion scrambled back, although there were doubts as to whether he had done so in time. But French referee Alfred Azaro, making his debut at this level, judged that he had and allowed the pounding to continue. It was a dreadful round for Benn, who scarcely landed a blow, but as the bell sounded he shook his head defiantly at the American.

> **"It was an astonishing display of sheer, bloody-minded courage, and McClellan had seen nothing like it before. He was used to opponents obligingly crumpling at his feet, and you could sense the subtle shifts in his mood from arrogance to panic and, finally, to desperation."**

The hammering continued for round after round, with Benn frequently teetering on the edge of defeat only to pull himself together and charge at McClellan, fists flailing. It was an astonishing display of sheer, bloody-minded courage, and McClellan had seen nothing like it before. He was used to opponents obligingly crumpling at his feet, and you could sense the subtle shifts in his mood from arrogance to panic and, finally, to desperation.

When Benn went down in the eighth, only to jump up and rock the challenger with a right hook, a lot of the heart seemed to drain from McClellan. He was fighting with his mouth open, constantly pushing his gumshield back in, and his nose was bleeding. His self-belief was trickling away by the second, and it finally seemed to run out in the 10th when he sank to one knee, from no punch in particular, and waited there while Azaro counted him out. In fact, something much more dreadful was happening behind McClellan's glazed eyes. A few minutes later he slid off his stool and lay unconscious on the canvas for around fifteen minutes while desperate attempts were made to revive him. He was rushed off for emergency brain surgery, which saved his life. But he will never again hear the roar of a crowd: blind and brain-damaged, he lives in a world of his own where he is still training for the next fight, and where he is still the undefeated champion.

Opposite and this page: Benn showed courage beyond belief to keep going despite taking a dreadful beating from the big-hitting American, including a knockdown in the eighth round (left).

CLASSIC FIGHTS

EVANDER HOLYFIELD

MIKE TYSON

WBA heavyweight title, Las Vegas, 9 November 1996

I**T was a result to restore faith in the sport**, an astonishing, logic-defying upset which proved once and for all that heavyweight championship boxing is on the level. Mike Tyson's defeat in the MGM Garden arena cost him, at a conservative estimate, $100m – and his promoter, the supposedly all-powerful Don King, lost at least as much again. Evander Holyfield was not supposed to give him a decent test, let alone beat him: in fact, there was serious and genuine concern for the veteran ex-champion's well-being and even his survival.

After all, Holyfield had looked like an old, shot fighter when losing to Riddick Bowe a year previously, while Tyson had steamrollered all four comeback opponents and recaptured two of the assorted versions of the world title (he later relinquished the WBC belt). Of 47 international journalists polled by a local paper before the fight, only one – Boston writer Ron Borges – picked Holyfield, and most expected him to be stopped. Borges, alone, gave proper consideration to two vital factors: the bottomless well of the challenger's courage and self-belief, and the possibility that Tyson might flounder when faced with a man he could not intimidate.

That is exactly what happened. Tyson tried to sweep Holyfield aside, but Evander stood head-to-head with him, absorbed the best Tyson could throw, and hit him back just as hard. At first we thought it was just the proud last stand of a big-hearted battler, but slowly the realization grew – in Tyson as well as the watchers – that Holyfield's challenge was real, and that this was one opponent who would not roll over as soon as Tyson snarled at him.

In the champion's corner, which lacked a seasoned strategist, concern quickly turned to panic as, unable to devise an alternative tactic, they watched their man begin to crumble. Holyfield, inexorably, took control, and underlined his superiority by flooring Tyson heavily in the sixth round. Yet for all his character deficiencies, Tyson has never lacked courage: this was no cowering bully who would fold at the first sign of resistance. He fought his heart out, trying with mounting desperation to turn the fight his way.

It was all to no avail. Holyfield outfought him and out-thought him, breaking him up bit by bit until, as the 10th round ended, the fighter who was once the most terrifying man in the business was reduced to a stumbling, beaten wreck. A dozen or so punches into the 11th round, it was over. Holyfield had pulled off one of the greatest shocks in boxing history, and the myth of Iron Mike was dead.

"At first we thought it was just the proud last stand of a big-hearted battler, but slowly the realization grew – in Tyson as well as the watchers – that Holyfield's challenge was real, and that this was one opponent who would not roll over as soon as Tyson snarled at him."

Tyson held his own in the early rounds (opposite) but was floored in the sixth (below) and by the 11th round (left) was a beaten man.

THE ARENAS

From the plush Victorian grandeur of London's Albert Hall to the sparsely functional York Hall in Bethnal Green, from the opulence of the MGM Garden Arena in Las Vegas to the aircraft-hanger austerity of Wembley Grand Hall in London – they all have their stories, and they have all hosted some of boxing's unforgettable events. The settings may vary dramatically, but the atmosphere in a fight arena is unmistakable and unique to the sport.

A. J. LIEBLING, boxing's most eloquent chronicler, wrote a memorable piece for the *New Yorker* about a fight show he attended in Tunis in 1956. 'Inside the building', he noted, 'there was precisely the same atmosphere as at the Sunnyside Gardens in Queens or the Central Sporting Club in the Faubourg Saint-Denis. Prize-fighting everywhere, like carnal love in the old story, is just like in Cincinnati.'

The Small Halls

He was right, in so far as he was talking about minor halls like those he mentioned or, in British terms, places like Shoreditch Town Hall or York Hall, Bethnal Green. In such venues, the atmosphere grows in intensity in direct proportion to the knowledge and commitment of the spectators: often the participants will be known personally to a sizeable percentage of the audience, which guarantees a decent decibel level. But the small halls – 'fight clubs' in American idiom – are an endangered species. Television has virtually killed them off, since purse levels have, thanks to TV input, risen to figures which are simply uneconomic for promoters to pay if they are wholly dependent for profit on the 800 or 1,000 fans who pay at the door.

Fight night at the Albert Hall, one of boxing's most atmospheric venues.

Shoreditch, also immortalized by Liebling in another *New Yorker* piece in 1957, closed its doors to boxing more than twenty years ago, yet for those old enough to remember the monthly and sometimes fortnightly shows there, it remains the definitive model of a classic small hall. It was tiny, seating around 800, with a balcony so low and intimate that it almost felt as though you could reach down and touch the top rope of the ring. The fighters were nearly always local, with their own passionate followings, and the very nature of the shows and the inaccessible location meant that the ticket-buyers were all knowledgeable, seasoned *aficionados* of the fight game. Shoreditch was never the fashionable place to be seen, and the Beautiful People gave it a very wide berth.

For genuine fight fans, though, that was precisely the attraction. Because the clientele were so well informed about the fare on offer, the promoters and their match-makers knew they could never get away with giving the favoured 'house fighters' the kind of easy knockovers they might expect on a bigger show at Wembley or the Albert Hall, before a less expert and therefore uncritical audience. Shoreditch punters demanded and got

James Toney beats Tim Littles on the evening in March 1994 when the Olympic Auditorium in Los Angeles reopened after a lengthy closure for refurbishment.

competitive, well-matched fights, and often the sheer intensity of the atmosphere in the hall lifted ordinary performers to unexpected heights of effort and achievement. It was at Shoreditch that Dick Tiger was paid £75 to stop Terry Downes, who earned £125, in the main event in May 1957: at various times in 1962, they each held a version of the world middleweight title. It was here that matchmakers like Mickey Duff and his successor Terry Lawless learned their trade, and practised the skills which, when used in a wider market, brought Britain a string of world champions in the 1970s and 1980s.

The crowd there could be generous to a brave loser, and 'nobbins' (showers of silver coins tossed into the ring in appreciation of a fine effort) were a feature of virtually every show. But they could also be wittily, wickedly sharp with non-triers. It was at Shoreditch, during a dreary six-rounder between a pair of reluctant warriors, that I saw a man in the balcony stand up, do an exaggerated stretch and yawn, and announce loudly 'Ah, well, put the light out – I'm off to bed.' Instantly, from the facing balcony, a voice answered 'Don't you dare put that light out – I'm trying to read the paper.'

In boxing's hey-day in the post-war boom, London used to have dozens of shows every month, but now the only small halls still functioning regularly are York Hall and the Elephant & Castle Leisure Centre. York Hall is used by all four of the main promoters, either as a low-budget 'studio' for televised shows or, rarely, as a hall where the promoter's novice talent can gather experience without the pressure of publicity. Because it is used equally by the various promoters, just about every leading British boxer has appeared there at some stage in their careers. World heavyweight title claimants Henry Akinwande, Herbie Hide and Lennox Lewis have boxed there. So have world champions Dennis Andries, Nigel Benn, Chris Eubank, Lloyd Honeyghan, Alfred Kotey, Eamonn Loughran, Duke McKenzie, Colin McMillan, Chris Pyatt and Steve Robinson, as well as virtually every British champion of the recent past.

Royal Albert Hall and Wembley Arena

Of the two major London venues, the circular, plush-seated Albert Hall was always more atmospheric than the vast and featureless Wembley Arena, although both have long associations with the sport. The Albert Hall hosted Jimmy Wilde's famous fight with Pete Herman in 1921, when Wilde only agreed to concede weight to the American when he was told that the Prince Of Wales was at ringside and would be disappointed if he didn't box. Wilde would have been better advised to tell the Prince to mind his own business: Herman battered him to a painful 17th-round defeat.

Nine years later, in the same ring, Jack 'Kid' Berg suffered similar aristocratic interference but had the good sense to ignore it. He was challenging the American Mushy Callahan for the world junior welterweight (10st) title, a division not recognized in Britain, when Lord Lonsdale interrupted the MC's introductions by striding down to ringside brandishing his cane and shouting 'There is no such championship.' Berg got on with his job, and stopped his man in the 10th round.

The famous old Kensington hall also hosted Teddy Baldock's two fights in 1927 for the British version of the world bantamweight title, when he beat Archie Bell and lost to Willie Smith, and it saw the coronation of WBC featherweight champions Howard Winstone and Johnny Famechon in 1968 and 1969. The Albert Hall's central location and comfort made it infinitely preferable to the long trek to Wembley, but Wembley's greater capacity (almost 11,000 compared to around 4,500) meant that it was the preferred venue for world title fights, especially in the days when gate receipts were paramount.

The first world title fight there has a unique footnote in boxing history, as the only occasion on which the matchmaker matched himself with a world champion. Len Harvey had been engaged by the arena's owner, Arthur Elvin, to serve as matchmaker and promptly paired himself with light-heavyweight champion John Henry Lewis in a title fight. Harvey was outpointed in an entertaining 15-rounder, and Wembley went on to host some memorable championships.

Benny Lynch, Walter McGowan and Charlie Magri won the flyweight title here; Terry Downes took the middleweight title from Paul Pender in 1961, three years before the great Emile Griffith outscored Welsh hope Brian Curvis in a welterweight title defence. John Conteh won the WBC light-heavyweight belt in 1974, and two years later the Wembley fans winced as Carlos Palomino took John Stracey's WBC welterweight title with some savage body punches.

Madison Square Garden

In pre-television America, Madison Square Garden was the Mecca of boxing. The original Garden, in the New York square which gave it its name, was an abandoned train shed that William K. Vanderbilt took over and renamed in 1879. John L. Sullivan was the first major name to appear there, and he also headlined the opening show of the second Garden, built in 1890 on the site of its predecessor. Champions like James J. Corbett, Bob Fitzsimmons, Terry McGovern, Joe Walcott and Jim Jeffries followed him there, along with later stars like Freddie Welsh, Willie Ritchie, Johnny Dundee and Sam Langford. The last show was held there on 5 May 1925, and on 11 December in the

Right and below: Caesars Palace, Las Vegas – still in a class of its own as a fight setting.

same year Paul Berlanbach outpointed Jack Delaney for the light-heavyweight title in the opening show of the latest Garden, built by promoter Tex Rickard at 49th and 8th Avenue a few miles uptown.

Under Rickard, Madison Square Garden became the undisputed headquarters of the sport, and a fighter had not 'arrived' until he had topped the bill there. Benny Leonard, Tony Canzoneri, Harry Greb, Max Schmeling, Jack 'Kid' Berg, Ruby Goldstein, Ray Robinson, Joe Louis, Rocky Marciano – all the stars among several generations of boxers were featured in the Garden, and on the nights when there was no boxing, the circus or the rodeo, the horse show or ice hockey matches took over.

Finally, the old building outlived its usefulness and a magnificent new arena was erected, above Penn Station on 7th Avenue. It opened with one of the greatest fights in boxing history – Joe Frazier's defeat of Muhammad Ali in March 1971 – and the following year launched the championship reign of the astonishing Roberto Duran, who won the lightweight title there from Scotland's Ken Buchanan and still commanded a world ranking 25 years later.

'Razor' Ruddock is beaten by Mike Tyson at the Mirage, one of Las Vegas's newest venues.

Las Vegas

However, two factors combined to oust even this superb arena from its position as the sport's premier venue – the explosion in television interest in boxing in the early 1970s, and the rise of Las Vegas as an international holiday and leisure centre. The owners of the Vegas casinos quickly made the connection between good fights and punters: the first would bring in the second. And they were happy to take the commercial risk out of promoting by paying the promoters a 'site fee' to bring the fight to their arena. It made sound business sense for everyone involved: the casinos quickly recouped their outlay on the tables and slots, the promoters were guaranteed a profit, the fighters earned handsomely, and the fans were able to enjoy a weekend's gambling as well as watching the fight.

There was heavy competition among the casinos, but Caesars Palace claimed and kept the top spot. They built a 17,000-seat open-air arena behind the casino – good weather is guaranteed in Nevada – and because of the arena's amphitheatre-style construction, managed to convey the intimacy of a smaller setting while ensuring that every customer had an unimpeded view. A string of classic fights were staged there involving ring legends like Larry Holmes, Marvin Hagler, Ray Leonard and Thomas Hearns, as Caesars spent lavishly to bring in the best.

As new casinos like the Mirage and the MGM opened, they elbowed into the market. Don King made a mutually profitable deal with the MGM to stage Mike Tyson's comeback fights there, and he also featured Julio Cesar Chavez in that fighter's series with Frankie Randall. The MGM Grand Garden, an indoor arena, can justifiably claim to be the world's plushest fight venue, but it has yet to establish the pedigree that marks Caesars out from the rest.

The Olympic, Los Angeles

Further west, in Los Angeles, the Olympic Auditorium was once that city's equivalent of London's Shoreditch Town Hall, a compact, purpose-built hall erected to host the boxing competition in the 1932 Olympic Games. As the city's demography changed, the Auditorium became the fighting heart of the Latino quarter, staging regular shows in which fierce Mexican rivalries were settled. The tradition endured into the 1980s, but the arena acquired an unhappy reputation when, in the space of three years, it was the setting for two tragedies linked by a bizarre coincidence. In September 1980, Johnny Owen of Wales was fatally injured in the 12th round of a bid for the WBC bantamweight title against Lupe Pintor. In September 1983, Francisco 'Kiko' Bejines suffered the same fate when he, too, was stopped in the 12th round by Alberto Davila, in a fight for the vacant WBC bantamweight title. In recent times the Olympic has fallen into disuse, partly because the area in which it is located is considered unsafe for visitors. Bob Arum attempted to revive it using Oscar De La Hoya as the bait, but abandoned the venture.

The Inglewood Forum in California enjoyed a golden era in the 1970s when featherweight rivals Danny Lopez, Ruben Olivares, David Kotey and Bobby Chacon engaged in their memorable round-robins, but it, too, is no longer in regular use as a major venue.

Elsewhere, the fortunes of famous arenas tend to be linked to a particular fighter: middleweight legend Carlos Monzon made Luna Park familiar to fight fans everywhere, while his Italian rival Nino Benvenuti enjoyed his greatest nights in Rome's Palazzo Della Sport. The King's Hall, Belfast will always be associated with Barry McGuigan, while Glasgow's Kelvin Hall was worth a three-rounds start to WBC lightweight king Jim Watt. In the end, it is the fights that matter, not the arenas: the stars have a way of shining in any setting.

Picture Credits

Action Plus: 85 (bttm)

Agence Vandystadt: Gerard Planchenault 42 (bttm)/Laurent Zabulon 49 (top)

Allsport: 7, 15 (bttm right), 31 (bttm), 67 (bttm)/Holly Stein 4 (bttm), 22, 24, 29, 31 (top), 42 (top), 68/ Steve Powell 5, 10, 20, 30, 33 (main), 36, 37, 85 (top)/Al Bello 11, 23 (bttm)/Bob Martin 13, 69 (top)/ Russell Cheyne 16 (left)/John Gichigi 16 (right), 17 (left), 40, 43 (top), 44 (bttm), 46 (bttm), 47 (bttm), 88, 89 (top)/Tony Duffy 21/Steve Dunn 25 (top), 43 (bttm), 50 (top)/ Mike Powell 27/ Mike Cooper 48 (top), 54/Ken Levine 87 (top), 95/Ben Radford 89 (bttm)

Allsport USA: 1/Al Bello 3, 45 (top), 49 (bttm), 50 (bttm), 90, 91 (bttm), 93/ Mike Powell 4 (middle), 25 (bttm)/Holly Stein 15 (bttm left), 17 (right), 18, 23 (top), 45 (bttm), 51 (both), 69 (bttm), 70/Jed Jacobsohn 34, 35 (top), 91 (top)/Ken Levine 35 (bttm), 87 (bttm)/Jim Gund 46 (top)/ David Leah 47 (top)/Simon Bruty 48 (bttm)

Associated Press: 73

***Boxing News*:** 77 (top), 79

Colorsport: 15 (top right), 32, 33 (inset), 44 (top)/Dan Helms 28

Corbis-Bettman/UPI: 38, 39 (both), 63 (both), 78, 83 (both)/the *Evening Standard* (UK) 26

Hulton Deutsch/The Allsport Historical Collection 4 (top), 52, 56, 58, 59 (bttm), 60, 61 (both), 64, 65 (bttm), 66, 67 (top), 76,

Popperfoto: 9, 55 (both), 57 (both), 59 (top), 62, 65 (top), 75, 77 (bttm), 94 (both)

***Ring Magazine*:** 80, 81 (both)

Sporting Pictures (UK): 12, 15 (top left), 92

Every effort has been made to trace the copyright holders and we apologize in advance for any unintentional errors or omissions. We would be pleased to insert the appropriate acknowledgement in any subsequent edition of this publication.